CARING FOR THE SMALL CHURCH

INSIGHTS FROM WOMEN IN MINISTRY

NANCY T. FOLTZ

Foreword by
Carl S. Dudley

**Douglas Alan Walrath
General Editor**

Judson Press ® Valley Forge

Bible quotations in this volume are from the *New Revised Standard Version* copyrighted 1989 by the Division of Christian Education of the National Council of the Churches of Christ in the United States of America, and are used by permission. All rights reserved.

Library of Congress Cataloging-in-Publication Data
Foltz, Nancy T.
Caring for the small church: insights from women in ministry/by
Nancy Foltz.
p. cm. —(Small church in action)
Includes bibliographical references.
ISBN 0-8170-1175-7
1. Small churches. 2. Women clergy. I. Title. II. Series.
BV637.8.F65   1993
253'.082—dc20   93-15844

Printed in the United States of America.

Contents

90094

Foreword

My wife and I both are employed in McCormick Theological Seminary in Chicago, Illinois, where she is the Registrar and I am Professor of Church and Community. When she falls behind in records and paperwork because she has too many interruptions, I knowingly suggest, "Just close your office door until you catch up on your work." She responds with equal firmness, "I can't close the door on people who come by—they *are* my work."

Although she is the record keeper and I am the teacher, gender more than job description shapes the way we do our jobs. She uses her relational skills to keep good records, while I am more inclined to shut the door and think my way through a course of study.

Nancy Foltz offers wonderful insights at the intersection between the gifts of gender and the responsibilities of pastoral leadership. This double-barreled book provides helpful handles to understand better both the dynamics of small congregations and the experiences of women in ministry.

In a writing style consistent with her content, Professor Foltz offers more stories than conceptual analysis. She speaks from within the experiences of women clergy and members of small churches. She does not equate the two, or suggest that all women or all small churches fit a particular mold. Rather, she shows numerous ways that each can develop and strengthen the gifts of the other.

Women and men may read this book for different reasons. Women may be affirmed by the experiences of other women in ministry. Men may read these pages to understand better a once-familiar world that now looks significantly different when seen through women's lenses. Men and women alike will be educated and challenged by previously unspoken insights from women in ministry.

By articulating these experiences of women in ministry, the book revisits old questions with fresh light, and exposes other questions that may have been ignored, or simply asked so long ago that they have lost their cutting edge. Frequently the structure of the argument is as important as each particular point. Stories, for example, are not used as anecdotes to support the argument, but serve as primary carriers of insight. With this shift of priorities, rational analysis becomes midrash upon the primary, lived text of pastor and people in ministry together.

Congregational studies, the second major emphasis of the book, come into focus through the experiences of women in ministry. Missing is the heavy emphasis on program, process, and "getting it right." Rather, readers are aware of the importance of silence and the playfulness of ritual, of intentional and habitual acts of worship, of the physical and spiritual dimensions of space. Church studies made by men, such as the congregational stories of James F. Hopewell, are set to the music of these women's perspectives. The familiar marks of the church remain, but they are seen through a different lens.

Finally, when compared with many parish books, readers of Nancy Foltz should be prepared to move at a more comfortable pace. Each chapter writes its own stories and offers unique lenses to refract the congregational experience. As if offering intellectual shelter and a cool moment for reflection, each chapter concludes with a guided exercise to grasp more fully the implications of that perspective. Like a good counselor, the author provides unhurried space for the reader to absorb and move on from one section to the next.

In their warm invitation to understand small churches from experiences of women, we should engage this book as a significant conversation with the author and her friends in ministry.

Carl S. Dudley

A Word About the Series

Small churches are in a class by themselves. To overlook their uniqueness is to misunderstand them.

Unfortunately, small churches are commonly misunderstood. For example, they have long been viewed as proving grounds for new pastors. According to that assumption beginning pastors should make their mistakes in small churches; fewer people are involved and, therefore, the mistakes will be less costly. Also, those who demonstrate their ability in ministry with small churches will likely be effective pastors of larger churches.

Such viewpoints are hardly warranted. Only the most crass perspective could hold that those who are members of small churches deserve consistently lower-quality, less-experienced pastoral care than those who are members of large churches. Small churches are not smaller versions of large churches. They are qualitatively, as well as quantitatively, different. The insights pastors gain in ministry with small congregations do not transfer directly to larger congregations. In my own experience those who minister well and are happy in a small church rarely are as happy or effective when they move to a large church. Church members who are nurtured and who are effective lay leaders in small churches rarely find similar nurture or are as able to serve when small churches become larger.

Small churches deserve to be dealt with in their own right. Denominational programs designed for large churches rarely suit the needs of small congregations. To draw the potential out of small congregations, those who lead them and who provide resources for them need to appreciate their potential as small churches.

This series of books is designed specifically for those who lead and support small churches. Each author is someone who cares about and understands the unique possibilities of small congregations.

The original plans for this series included a book that recognizes the unique insights, gifts, and concerns women bring to ministry with small churches. We are very pleased that Nancy Foltz accepted the invitation to write this book. Nancy knows the realities of pastoral ministry with small churches. She also has served as a United Methodist conference staff person charged with supporting those who minister with small churches, and for the past several years she has worked as an independent consultant. Nancy brings to this book sound theology, skills honed as a pastor and consultant, and long experience as a woman in ministry. The result is a challenging and insightful book that will be immensely helpful to all of us who care for and minister with small churches.

Douglas Alan Walrath
General Editor

Acknowledgments

So many women have contributed to this book that I cannot thank them all. I wish to offer to them my appreciation for their stories, their willingness to speak, and their friendships—with special thanks to Revs. Beverly James, Charlene H. Pierce, Lisa J. Lyon, Joanne Torma-Kelly, and Evelyn Bedell, and Sister Sheila Carney.

I am also grateful for the students at Pittsburgh Theological Seminary, who so willingly tell me their stories and share their ministry experiences with me.

In addition, my family—husband, Bob, and sons, Drayton and Nelson—have been sources of great encouragement.

Finally, my thanks to editor Doug Walrath, who offered me the opportunity to write. His willingness to allow the book to take on a life of its own is testimony to his openness and trust that somewhere in the journey through these pages, church leaders will find words that affirm, encourage, and give hope.

Introduction

"I am not looking for permission to quit; on the contrary, I am looking for signs of hope." —*Lisa*

I have written this book about clergywomen in the small church to encourage people like Lisa, a seminary student serving a small church who wrote these words in one of my classes. Ministry in the small church demands specific qualities of leadership, and over the years I have been intrigued by the ways in which clergy, and women clergy in particular, are shaping and being shaped by ministry in small churches.

For this writing, the definition of the small church includes those congregations with a membership of two hundred fifty or fewer members. The small church may be rural, urban, or suburban. Many churches began as small churches and have remained so; others were once large, downtown congregations who are coming to terms with shrinking memberships and are now recognizing that they share the characteristics of small churches.

In this book I do not present statistical data about small churches or a chronological history of women in ministry. Instead, I have gathered stories, reflected on them, and now relay them to you. Telling stories is one way of revealing what happens on the inside of ministry in the small church, and narrative discourse informs us in a way that analysis of hierarchies, structures, and denominational polity does not. Through listening to the stories of clergywomen, we will explore the fabric of ministry in the small church—how that ministry is designed, embroidered, and enjoyed, as well as how tangled threads and frayed seams are handled.

Chapter One, "Qualities of Leadership in the Small Church," identifies traits clergywomen bring to ministry in the small church. Chapter Two, "Caring for Your Spiritual Life," focuses on the spiritual life of church leaders in the midst of caring for others. In Chapter Three, "Rituals That Grace Ministry," we will examine the role of ritual in bringing freshness to preaching, teaching, and learning. And in Chapter Four, "Parish World View," we will define four world views and consider their impact on relationships between the congregation and pastor. Questions for reflection and conversation are included at the end of each chapter for individual or group use.

My intent in writing this book is to offer both women and men involved in ministry in the small church the opportunity to hear what others have felt and experienced. My hope is that their stories will encourage and support many others, including women like Lisa, who are called to ministry in the small church.

Chapter 1

Qualities of Leadership in the Small Church

Far into the night, while the other creatures slept, Charlotte worked on her web. First she ripped out a few of the orb lines near the center. She left the radial lines alone, as they were needed for support. As she worked, her eight legs were a great help to her. So were her teeth. She loved to weave, and she was an expert at it.

from *Charlotte's Web* by E. B. White

If you have ever watched a spider at work, you have probably been amazed at the intricate webs these small creatures can make. I have watched webs blow and swing in a storm. Although they look delicate, spider webs are incredibly strong and not easily torn apart or broken.

Women and men in leadership in the small church must also be "web wise." Like those of the spiders, the "web" of the small church is intricate and strong and able to weather many storms, though it may appear delicate. Leaders in small churches must be able to identify the weakest and most dangerous points on which to tread. They must know and trust that the strength of the web is drawn from its interconnectedness.

In this chapter we will identify some of the specific qualities of leadership most needed in the small church—qualities that women in particular often bring to ministry. I have worked with numerous clergy in small churches over the past twenty years. I have listened to the stories of women and men in my seminary classes who are serving small churches; I have listened to the stories of women who are serving and who have served small churches. The leadership qualities that surface in their stories are those that often have not been recognized as "real" qualities

1

of leadership, qualities such as sharing information and authority, caring, and being accessible. In my experience these qualities
are found in women more often than in men at this point in the
church's history. Since such qualities are essential for small-
church ministry, where laypersons often put a high value on
these skills and ministries, women clergy have a distinct advantage in the small church—and men have a great learning opportunity to develop qualities not always valued for men in our
society.

Several studies of the leadership qualities of women have in-
formed my thinking on ministry in the small church. John Naisbitt and Patricia Aburdene conclude in their book, *Reinventing
the Corporation,* that "women can transform the workplace by expressing, not by giving up, their personal values."[1] Naisbitt and
Aburdene suggest that culturally we have separated genders in
the workplace and the consequence of that separation is that we
have "become blind to genuine abilities each possesses,"[2] thus
limiting our collective capabilities. In their new book, *Megatrends
for Women: Women Are Changing the World,* Naisbitt and Aburdene
conclude that women in positions of leadership are transforming
the world as well as the workplace, and they make numerous
references to the work of Sally Helgesen as significant in uncov-
ering the new way women prefer to lead and manage.[3]

The findings from Sally Helgesen's intriguing research de-
tailed in her book, *The Female Advantage: Women's Ways of Leading,*
undergird the stories I have heard from women clergy. I believe
that what Helgesen discovered about female leaders in the workplace can be applied to clergy as well: women are distinct from
men in the way they lead and minister in the church. Helgesen
asserts that traits and qualities of leadership are not gender ex-
clusive, however; rather, our culture and institutions have
blessed and given credibility to certain leadership styles and not
to others.

Helgesen studied four successful leaders: Frances Hesselbein,
national executive director of the Girl Scouts; Barbara Grogan,
president of Western Industrial Contractors; Nancy Badore, director of Ford Motor Company's Executive Development Center;
and Dorothy Brunson, president of Brunson Communications.
She found that these women functioned strongly at the level of
relationship and process. She reports that they repeatedly used
words such as flow, interaction, access, conduit, involvement,
network, and reach. "These are words," Helgesen explains,
"that above all emphasize relationships with people; they are

also *process* words that reveal a focus on the doing of various tasks rather than on the completion."[4]

The 1990 Helgesen study parallels management scientist Henry Mintzberg's 1968 doctoral study of male leadership, but with significant differences. Mintzberg examined the daily routines of five male managers and his diary studies provided the method that Helgesen used, but Helgesen used narratives that give a picture of the female leader, rather than Mintzberg's lists of tasks. Helgesen's work also studied each of the four women in terms of their personalities and histories, selecting two executives and two entrepreneurs, while Mintzberg studied only male executives in management positions. Helgesen's concern in writing was "to discover how women are changing the workplace" rather than studying only *corporate* women.[5]

In her study Helgesen identified eight characteristics about the way in which women functioned as leaders, each of which was compared to Mintzberg's characteristics of male leadership. For our purposes we will focus only on Helgesen's findings about women. They are:

1. The women worked at a steady pace, but with small breaks scheduled in throughout the day.
2. The women did not view unscheduled tasks and encounters as interruptions.
3. The women made time for activities not directly related to their work.
4. The women preferred live action encounters, but scheduled time to attend to mail.
5. They maintained a complex network of relationships with people outside their organizations.
6. They focused on the ecology of leadership.
7. They saw their own identities as complex and multifaceted.
8. The women scheduled in time for sharing information.[6]

From these eight findings we can identify five distinct qualities of leadership that women bring to their work in the small church:

1. Sharing as a deliberate process.
2. Paying attention to the larger context.
3. Being accessible.
4. Using pieces of time.
5. Recognizing our multifaceted identity.

Men may also identify with some or all of these qualities of leadership. My intent here is not to elevate either women or men or to assert that these qualities are gender-based. Rather, I wish to explore how each of these five qualities might transfer as strengths of ministry in the small church for both women and men, and to consider the implications of these qualities of leadership in light of the experiences of clergywomen serving in small churches.

1. Sharing as a deliberate process.

The management of information is an important aspect of any leadership position. Helgesen's study revealed a number of distinctions concerning the sharing of information by women, and the role these women assumed in its dissemination. The women chose to share information rather than to collect or hoard it, and they deliberately scheduled specific times with colleagues for the purpose of information exchange.

The notion of leadership inherent in this process of information sharing is that the women viewed themselves "as being in the center of things rather than at the top; it's more natural to reach *out* than to reach *down.* "[7] Think of the metaphors women often use: *web, dance, circle.* These are quite different from the more competitive or hierarchical images more commonly used by men, such as *climbing the ladder, battleground,* or *goal post.* The leader's location in relation to others during the process of exchanging or sharing information is significant in understanding leadership style.

Implications for the Small Church

Unfortunately, a leadership style that is grounded in the sharing of information and leadership roles is often mistaken as weakness. When a pastor hesitates in answering the question, "What do you think we need to be doing?" the congregation may conclude that she is weak or indecisive. On the contrary, she may be choosing not to answer because she knows that a congregation's investment, ownership, and participation in ministry begins with group or local-leader investment, not with her opinions.

Inviting outside resource leaders to come and share information is a critical task of the small-church pastor, despite the personal and professional risk involved in deliberately sharing leadership authority in the church. For example, one clergywoman lamented to me: "Last week a stewardship consultant from our denominational headquarters came to talk to some of our folks. As I listened to his suggestions, I thought, there isn't anything my people are hearing that I have not said to them over the past two years. I went away a bit depressed because my leaders were interested in this consultant's stewardship ideas but could not hear mine."

This is a typical situation in which the pastor suggests a good idea but the congregation is not ready or able to hear it; as time passes, the same idea is suggested by someone else and accepted. This clergywoman need not view such a scenario as failure on her part, though, but as a major accomplishment. Her openness to information sharing from denominational headquarters led to the congregation's ability to move forward and grow in Christ.

Information sharing among congregations and denominational leaders is critical in building a broad leadership base in a congregation. The challenge to clergy in the small church is to find ways of including rather than excluding others who have information to share. Clergy need to encourage that sharing in the form of stories, for the telling of personal, local needs and opportunities for ministry is the most effective means of communicating in the small church. And clergy need to help create new boundaries for ministry where sharing can expand beyond the congregation and community.

When the sharing of information is part of the life of the faith community, we hear statements such as "Frank Jones is out of work, and we need to help him out financially until he gets back on his feet." When members of the congregation begin to share as a deliberate process they may become vulnerable by exposing places in their lives where they are in need of help. Responding to the needs of members and persons in the community is often a way of enlarging the ministry. The small church's resources expand as its members share. According to author Carl Dudley, a small group functions as a family—a single-cell, history-bearing, culture-carrying unit.[8] A family shares with their own and often with others as well.

The small-church family builds in a "time for sharing" during the service, at a meeting, anytime they come together. During the service there is probably a time, for instance, when Ruth can stand and give us the news that "Martha and Harold reached their daughter Jane's house just fine. I know that many of you worried because of the weather last Friday night." This time of sharing is critical because it is an occasion of both affirmation and participation. During a time of sharing, the faith community affirms who they are as a people of God. They tell the story of how each takes care of the other. Sharing time is also an opportunity for individuals to participate in the service and to care for and reach out to one another.

It can be interesting to observe the cycles and patterns of information sharing that the congregation models. Clergy might want to record these "times of sharing" over the course of a three-month period and observe the patterns that emerge. Are the same folks always sharing, or are others telling new stories about new ways of caring?

The sharing of information and leadership by clergy is often viewed by women as part of the process of "reaching out" rather than "reaching down." Asking for conversation on an issue, describing ministry as in the community and as a part of our congregation's mission, preaching about the world as a place in which we live and have responsibility is the language of "reaching out."

"When I knew I was moving to Stanton, I said in my interview, 'I am in ministry with you, and I need each person to do what you have been doing and to help me understand the ministry you have.' " This clergywoman expressed a desire to extend the leadership circle beyond herself as a way of leading. "Reaching out" is often misinterpreted as a sign of weakness, but in reality, "reaching down" is more a sign of weakness because it involves commanding and directing rather than engaging and challenging others. If clergy are to develop lay leaders in the church, then they must reach out to extend the circle of leaders.

When I ask church members to draw a circle representing their small church and to mark an X somewhere on the paper to indicate the place of their pastor, they often place the pastor outside the church circle.[9] A wise leader knows that exercising effective leadership in small groups, units, and families is a slow, deliberate, and delicate experience. Clergy leadership is tied to trust, to getting to know the congregation and letting themselves be known. Clergy should not presume themselves to be "at the top," "in control," or "in charge." Instead, they are working with others and in due time, if fortunate enough, they will be adopted by the lay leaders of their church. Adoption or acceptance by the lay leadership will move the clergy to the inside of the small church circle.

Reaching out in ministry has two dimensions: the personal leadership of the clergy, and the church's collective reaching out to minister to others. For clergy, reaching out involves their attitude toward others, acknowledging the gifts and experiences of others as significant. To reach out is to call forth the individual gifts and resources for the good of the faith community. It is about making available to the congregation opportunities that are not presently considered a part of the scope of its ministry. The sharing of information and leadership challenges the church community to redefine together the boundaries of their ministry.

It takes longer to reach out than to reach down, however, and often there is a time lag between the pastor's arrival and the pastor's being granted permission to reach out. Clergy can be disappointed when they find that being present physically, emotionally, spiritually, and mentally does not necessarily mean that lay members will respond to the ministries of reaching out that the clergy identify. Wise leaders know that ministry is a collective rather than an individual effort, and the ability to respond to challenges in the community and world are often ways to mark the progress of a congregation in their capacity to see needs beyond the walls of the church building.

The reaching out ministries of small churches are often poorly communicated. The unfortunate reality is that many people beyond the congregation are unaware of the ministries of the small church. In a time of downsizing, when mainline denominational headquarters are looking for ways to reduce costs, cut unnecessary programs, and save leadership energy, the threat to the small church is real. The wider church needs to know of the vital ministries of the small churches in their communities and world.

Small-church ministries are diverse and practical, and grants can help make such ministries available when financial support is a problem. For example, prison kits for women entering the Missouri Correctional Institution, "Readin' & Writin' Pacs" for elementary children, personal hygiene kits for emergency shelters and shelters for the homeless, "Baby Bundles" for the newborn in low-income families—all have been developed and delivered since 1987 through the Festival of Sharing ministry.[10] Local churches can also participate in broader projects such as Heifer Project International and Habitat for Humanity.

Various ecumenical configurations also present new options for ways of providing pastoral leadership in small churches. Juanita Roberts came to love pastoring a variety of churches in a rural area, where she travels as far as a hundred miles from home to make her hospital calls.[11] Her reaching out extends into the wider community and beyond. Through her ministry, various denominational churches are being served, creating a unified ministry with diverse gifts.

Sharing as a deliberate process can work well in the small church because ministry in the small church is based on the principle that families share. Often a member of the church tells others about the need, and they will then decide together how to respond. The small church must be more deliberate in the sharing of what is ministry and how is ministry reaching out to members, the community, and the world. One of the contributions of clergy must be the clear communication in the congregation and in the denomination and beyond about the ministry of the small church. Telling the story is a central leadership issue in sharing as a deliberate process.

2. Paying attention to the larger context.

The women in Helgesen's study maintained a long-range, "big-picture" vision of the society in which they performed their leadership roles. They were conscious of themselves as "participants in a revolution in expectations of and opportunities for women."[12] Helgesen also found that women leaders were deeply aware of the interrelatedness of all the different aspects of their work, of their lives, and of the society in which they lived. Their "ecology of leadership"—leadership that takes in the whole context as well as its parts—included focusing on the day-to-day operation of their businesses as well as on a larger vision for the future.

These qualities of leadership translate well into the small church, where there are multiple centers of people, activities, and ideas that are all interrelated. Small-church ministry is relational in every way, and when one relationship is out of order the whole system of interpersonal exchanges is affected. One decision about finances affects other forthcoming decisions that will also need funding. If the church leadership is out of sorts with the denomination, that disgruntled attitude will affect other parts of the small church's ministry. In the small church, the ecology of leadership identified in Helgesen's study means paying attention to the whole of ministry, anticipating how various parts affect the others and helping to make the necessary connections. Thus, the ecology of leadership in the small church often necessitates a proactive leadership role for clergy.

Implications for the Small Church

"I am the first female pastor for this charge," Susan told me. She is also the first single-parent pastor and the first divorced clergyperson to serve in her church. Susan is aware that her ministry not only in the congregation but also in the community and denomination is being closely observed; her work in this church will establish what happens in the future with her own ministry and that of clergywomen who will follow.

Many small-church clergywomen are well aware that they are "the first." More often than not, the clergywoman is a first not only for the church but also for the community. To serve in such a capacity, knowing that others will come after, and to lead in such a way that unjust systems can be changed, presents quite a challenge. It is particularly important, therefore, that the leader have an ecology of leadership, including a willingness to be herself and take time for her own development and for non-work related activities, and an ability to see the big picture of the church's ministry and how she is contributing to that ministry.

For women clergy today it is especially important to be attentive to the larger context of women in ministry. For example, one clergywoman in a small-church setting had served her five churches for six years, and denominational leaders were trying to convince her to move because her salary had reached the limit her churches could afford. She wanted to stay, and the churches wanted her to stay, but the denomination said she should be earning more and had to move on. Although she felt God calling her to serve those churches, she also needed to face the broader, professional issues of length of service, status, and salary from the perspective of a denomination. She decided to stay and continue to serve the five churches, while reminding the denomination that inequities in salary and location exist among clergy, and that clergy who are called to ministry in the small church must face financial concerns that their colleagues who move to larger churches with increased salaries do not encounter. Perhaps the time will come when denominations can offer a secure base salary, regardless of location for ministry, so that pastors can earn a fair wage and not be penalized for their call to the small church. Until that time, it will be important for this clergywoman to see the inequities she faces in the larger context of compensation for ministry in the church.

Where clergy live is also a part of the larger context of ministry. When clergy live in the community in which their small church is located, it is almost impossible to ignore the interrelatedness of major efforts in ministry. The Sunday school superintendent is also on the school board, and the trustees are also on the town council. Local community news and church news is exchanged often in the same conversation. In the small church, the ability to view life as interrelated and understanding the ecology of leadership is a definite advantage. The church, the community, the leaders historic and present—all work together toward unfolding a future. There is no map, no one way, no clear-cut direction for success in the small church. As a mother superior, addressing the faith community of two hundred as they began a two-year plan of financial accountability said, "Listen, pilgrim, there is no path, we make the path by walking."[13]

When there is no clear path, no "how-to" guidebook, then we must be fully attentive to the whys and hows of the journey. Understanding the small church begins with the historical questions of why a particular church does what it does. Often in asking the why questions we bump into the real values of a congregation. Then leaders are able to search for additional or alternative pathways for accomplishing the same objective. Creative clergy leaders often become bored with maintenance ministry or doing this year what they did last year and in just the same way. There is no "just one way to do this" route for the small church. By opening the possibilities of the larger context to the congregation and by gathering histories, sorting information, and planting ideas in new ways, ministries in the small church can continue to change and grow.

Providing leadership that includes paying attention to the larger context has numerous implications for ministry in the small church. In the American Indian tradition, leaders speak of preparing for seven generations to come and are encouraged to look over their shoulder and see the faces of sons and daughters of the future. Clergy must look both ways: over one shoulder to see the future generations, and over the other shoulder to remember the local history and tradition that shaped the congregation.

Interrelatedness in the small church means knowing that as you argue with Sue Davies, you are probably arguing with fourteen other persons in the congregation, since she is the daughter of John and the cousin of Mary, and on and on. Leaders in small churches need to develop a sensitivity to each teaching and learning moment. Sometimes the attentive clergy will simply learn about who is related to whom; other times she or he will learn about how complicated and sometimes difficult the living out of those relationships is in that church.

It is also important for pastors to recognize that natural and psychological boundaries exist in congregations. The natural boundaries may be mountains, rivers, the Henderson intersection, or a county line. The psychological boundaries may be such concerns as "How big we can get without losing our identity?" or "How many times we will join with 'the other church' for services?" or "How many sermons do we want to hear on mission?" Anyone coming into the community needs to be patient, to hear the stories and learn about how the people experience faith and Scripture.

The past rather than the future is more often the topic of conversation in small churches. Pastors need to listen to such conversations carefully. Knowing how historical changes occurred are clues as to how changes might come about tomorrow. If the church has not had a certain service for a particular historical reason, the pastor would be wise to look into the history before scheduling that service.

For example, the state fair, the Wilson Church, and the Maple Grove homecoming service are all historically connected. Pastor Carol tells of "a former resident of Warren County and a member of the congregation who promoted the local 4-H program. With his influence the program grew and involved a number of the children. Last year my daughter showed a lamb at the fair. Usually the first weekend of the fair, animals are shown, and on that weekend we don't have a service at Wilson Church. Most of the time this allows Maple Grove to have an eleven o'clock homecoming service."

If a pastor at Wilson Church were to insist on a service the weekend of the fair, it would be disruptive to the historical tradition. Uproot one tree in the forest and you affect all other trees; uproot one historical tradition and you uproot all others. Participating in the traditions and enhancing them when you can is helpful; uprooting traditions and trying to bring them to an end can be destructive. Pastors should not expect to change those traditions that are deeply rooted in the soil of local culture—but they need to understand them.

Just as pastors need to be aware of the interconnectedness of people and of the traditions that are important to them, they also need to be aware of the congregation's cultural values. The conflicts and misunderstandings that can arise in small churches because of differences in cultural values underlines the importance of maintaining a vision of the larger context of ministry. When we make decisions in the church, our choices are based on values we hold as a congregation. When we preach, the challenges we offer come from the basic values we embrace. When we teach, we are not speaking about unrelated truths or pieces of knowledge; we are transmitting core or basic values that underlie who we are as a people of God and why we respond in our lives as we do. It is our values as a congregation that help us know how to settle arguments, make financial commitments, and create new ministries.

Resources are available to church leaders who wish to broaden their understanding of the culture in which they serve; one of the clearest resources I have found is a book by Tex Sample called *U.S. Lifestyles and Mainline Churches.*[14] Sample suggests that the membership in the small church often consists primarily of people who are of the "cultural right": self-denying, local folks, mostly of the World War II generation. These are people who are rooted in their neighborhood communities, who are respectable and hard-working, who love their country and their church, and who tend to receive their faith primarily through the Bible and the spoken word. They develop a kind of "folk theology" that is profoundly biblical, deeply communal, and is expressed through story. In folk theology the purpose of telling a story is not to explain faith, but rather "to evoke what the heart already knows."[15] When folks in the small church are asked a question they often answer it by telling about a time when—and they begin to recount the story. Faith for them is a matter of the heart.

On the other hand, the mind-set of the clergywoman is probably either of the "cultural left" or the "cultural middle," for although the median age of the graduating seminarian is rising, we still have a majority of younger pastors serving small churches as their first church. These pastors are probably much younger than the congregation they are serving, perhaps a part of the baby-boomer generation with its intensely personal, strongly individualistic approach to religion and its radically different lifestyles that are highly mobile, business or professional in outlook, and tolerant of diversity. In addition, they often express their faith metaphorically rather than using "oughts" and "shoulds." These characteristics are typical of Tex Sample's profile of the cultural middle.

If a congregation carries predominantly cultural-right expectations representative of the dominant culture, what happens when the person in the pulpit is a woman who is not of the cultural-right perspective? The translation work required of the clergywoman of the cultural left or cultural middle would certainly include an acknowledgement of differences and some sense of how critical these differences are. For example, if a politically aware, self-fulfillment-oriented twenty-five-year-old clergywoman is serving a predominantly self-denying, traditional-lifestyle congregation, then the basic values that each holds as important would need to be clear. Questions about what values and beliefs guide the decisions and actions of the clergywoman and of the congregation would need to be discussed openly and honestly.

For example, the Bible knowledge of the cultural right and the cultural left may be worlds apart. But if the congregation can say, "She knows her Bible; that's one reason we get along with her," then they have identified a connecting bridge between the pew and the pulpit. If on the other hand they say, "She always challenges everything we ever believed," then there will be turmoil in the faith community. When the storytelling, folk-theology cultural-right member meets the cultural-left clergywoman at the sermon, the member may be listening for folk theology and the preacher may be preaching a socially conscious sermon.

Whenever individuals gather from different backgrounds there needs to be an attentiveness to language to avoid misunderstanding the messages being given. In small congregations, people who have been together over years have developed a way of communicating that often sounds like shorthand. They know how to give messages clearly to one another. When clergy come into the congregation they probably bring another language and other ways to give messages, and they cannot assume that the congregation will be able to hear clearly the messages they are trying to give. The reverse is also true: laypeople may not be sending messages in a language that the pastor is able to hear. Either way, the pastor and congregation need to create ways of checking to see if messages between the pulpit and the pew are being sent and received clearly and accurately.

This work of translation and clarity in communication is a vital part of leadership in the small church, especially when the situation is complicated by cultural differences and values. The leadership quality of maintaining a vision of the larger context in which ministry is offered can be essential to the process of adjusting to different ways of proclaiming the Gospel and of leading in the small church.

3. Being accessible.

A third quality of leadership Sally Helgesen identified in her study has to do with accessibility. The women in Helgesen's study made a deliberate effort to be accessible. Unscheduled tasks and encounters were not viewed as interruptions, because the women believed that spending time with people who were not scheduled into their day was related to being involved and responsible in their capacity as leaders. Many so-called female values, such as appreciating diversity and drawing on "personal, private sphere experience when dealing in the public realm," are "nurtured in the private, domestic sphere to which women have been restricted for so long."[16] In this sense, being accessible certainly falls into this category of "female values."

This quality of accessibility is clearly important in the leadership provided by clergy as well, especially in the small church. "In the middle of sermon preparation, the phone rang and Marie needed someone to listen," one clergywoman explains. "So I got in the car and drove to her house." There is no sense in this conversation that Marie should not have called or that the sermon would not get finished, but rather that Marie's request for time was equally a part of the clergywoman's ministry in that church. She knew that ministry often is a series of unscheduled tasks and interruptions.

When I worked with an order of Roman Catholic sisters, we would schedule full-community meeting days, when all two hundred sisters would come together from all over the United States. Several times when we met, someone would report that a sister had recently died in the mother house: "Sister Marie died this morning at six. Several of us were by her bedside from late yesterday afternoon. We sang her favorite hymns, we prayed with her, and we were present in the silences of her dying." These marvelous sisters understood what it means to be accessible, to stop what you are doing when something really important is occurring. They know that losing a night's sleep to be present with a dying sister *is* the ministry. Life in the community was not interrupted; schedules were altered to permit persons to be present to celebrate the ending of life on earth.

The "interruptibility factor"—that grace to stop what you are doing and care for the person before you who is in need—is a contribution women bring to ministry. Inherent in the nature of ministry is a need for flexibility, spontaneity, and accessibility. "When John died, I didn't know who else to call. I'm glad you were home," said one woman to her woman pastor.

Implications for the Small Church

Being accessible to those in need raises issues of boundaries for clergy and members of the congregation, and care must be given to guarding the clergyperson's need for personal time and space, for time away from the church. A story is told of Catholic author Henri Nouwen when he went away for a retreat. At the retreat house, several students, upon learning that Nouwen was present, requested that he lead them in a series of devotionals. Nouwen felt, however, that was his time for retreat and he ought not to interrupt his retreat to prepare for the students. The retreat director suggested to Nouwen that the preparation should not be difficult, for surely Nouwen in his faithfulness all these years could gather some devotional material for the students. After reflection, Nouwen chose to make himself accessible to the students for their retreat.

There are at least two central issues to this story. The first is the question of accessibility as it relates to personal time: knowing when to change a personal schedule, and knowing when and how to protect personal time. It is impossible for anyone to develop a hard and fast rule on the use of time and accessibility. The fact that the retreat director spoke to Nouwen about the students' request hints that there were differing expectations about Nouwen's accessibility that were not clarified before Nouwen entered the retreat setting. Clarifying expectations is essential in knowing how accessible people expect clergy to be. The amount of time needed to fulfill this request is also a critical element in the story. If the total retreat time had been requested I suspect that this unscheduled request would have been renegotiated or denied.

Accessibility in the small church will vary according to the expectations of individual churches and pastors. The number of one-to-one conversations a small church expects of its pastor tends to decrease as the size of the worshiping congregation increases. As a church grows and develops a more formal structure, with numerous chairpersons doing the work, there is less of an expectation that the pastor be known by and know each person.[17] The key is to be clear and explicit about those expectations.

Boundaries are set together as expectations are named. One task of the clergy is answering the congregation's question, "When you say you are available and accessible, what do you have in mind?" Each pastor needs to balance accessibility with the need for private space and personal time. "I saw the lights on in the parsonage, so I thought it was all right to call," some members of the congregation might say, believing that when the pastor is home, the pastor is available. On the other hand, Pastor Ellen's expectation was that folks would invite her to their homes: "I think that I have been invited to only four homes for a meal over the past three and a half years." Both pastor and congregation have boundaries and expectations that need to be identified and agreed upon in order for their ministry to grow.

By being accessible and listening to people's private stories, secrets no one else has heard, the pastor is placed in a high-level position of trust. One pastor had a parishioner stop in her office and tell her about her experience of being raped when she was eleven. "I've told my husband," the parishioner said. "You are the only other person I have told." The pastor later reflected on having heard this "family secret": "I benefitted because I was a female and I was there. This women had been in silence . . . like I was in silence until I found my voice. She is telling the family secrets. Once the truth starts to be told, everyone can get help. She privileged me to look into her private life." This particular pastor is well aware of the significance of being a good listener, and part of being a good listener is making oneself available, making the time to listen.

Being accessible and hearing family secrets carries the crucial obligation to confidentiality, credibility, and privacy. Since news spreads quickly over the small-church grapevine, pastors must be careful to guard information told to them in confidence. Ironically, there is another advantage to being accessible: as people confide in you, you are apt to learn fast who is on the grapevine and how it works.

In general, small churches are usually informal—and want the pastor to be also. Suggestions like "Why don't you call the office and make an appointment to see me?" may be offensive to some. Pastors who are loved by small congregations are usually those willing to be available in the grocery store and the post office as well as the church office. The highly relational nature of the small church encourages accessibility.

4. Using pieces of time.

When Helgesen looked at the use of time in her study of women leaders, she noted that the women worked at a steady pace and included small breaks throughout the day. They used language such as "snatching at little pieces of time" and "catching a breath" to describe this quality of purposefully using small units of time and intentionally pacing their days.

The notion of "snatching at little pieces of time" reminds me of continuous improvement. How do we create change? We create the new by constantly making small improvements. Making changes involves the ability to maintain a steady pace, keeping at something until it is done. Big jobs get done if you break them into smaller ones.

It is interesting that the emphasis on quality, which is so widespread throughout businesses today, includes the idea of working for fifty minutes and then taking a break for ten minutes. It seems as though women have already made use of this basic principle of taking breaks and pacing one's time.

Implications for the Small Church

The small church has a rhythm based more on cycles and swings than on clocks and calendars. Knowing when it's time to sit and have a cup of coffee and when it's time to finish putting together the bulletin is understanding "snatching at little pieces of time."

The smaller the community, town, or village, the more apt people are to have unwritten expectations about when the pastor should be up and moving in the morning and when is too late in the evening to go visiting. An unwritten expectation may be that our pastor is a "rise-and-shine" person. Getting up and about early in the community may give a positive signal. Knowing when to linger and when to move on is necessary in making good use of pieces of time.

In the small church, most often leadership is about Harold doing it rather than about Harold and a committee working on a project. Folks know that individuals do and committees usually don't. So conversation with Harold may come in three or six parts. One period of time may be on Sunday after church, another time on Tuesday at the gas station, and a third time on the street Saturday morning. This is effective "snatching at pieces of time."

It is important for leaders in small churches to realize that pacing can increase energy rather than deplete it. Knowing when to break and when to keep on going is the key to good energy flow. Working at a steady pace while knowing that you can leave the work for five minutes and come back to it usually increases energy. Deliberate pacing techniques, such as taking five minutes to read a favorite book, brew yourself a cup of special tea, or take a brisk walk around the block can ensure peace of mind. Clergywomen may be more adept at handling the flexible break that can come when least expected. Any clergywoman who works out of her home knows the benefit of putting in a load of laundry when there is a dry spell in her writing of the Sunday sermon. It isn't the laundry that breaks the dry spell; it is changing the environment, the mind-set, that often generates and stimulates new thought patterns.

I ask my small-church seminary class to jot down ten five-minute-or-less "treats" that they give themselves at low or no cost. Do they like to shut their eyes and relax? listen to some classical music? jog? read a few minutes in that enjoyable book? You might like to try writing down on paper ten of your "treats," and then marking those that you have given to yourself in the past two weeks. It can be harder to remember to take those breaks than one would think! Many of my students had denied themselves all of these small indulgences because they were sure they did not have time for them. But some acknowledged that they had taken a bubble bath or called a friend or read a short story—and that the small break had energized them.

There can also be incredible diversity in the way each lay leader in the small church works. For instance, some laypersons will assume individual responsibility rather than do work "by committee." Each will have his or her unique style of pacing, which will be important for the minister to understand. Some leaders will accomplish a great deal but never appear to be in a hurry. Obviously, they know something about pacing. Whether or not the work ethic is ingrained in the culture of your community, you have an opportunity to both model and learn new ways of pacing. Knowing how other leaders in the congregation pace themselves—and that your own pacing may be different—can be a strength in developing an effective ministry.

5. Recognizing our complex and multifaceted identity.

When the women in Helgesen's study spoke of the question of identity, they described their identities as complex and multifaceted. Whether they were single, married, parents, or community volunteers, all of these various roles were part of who they were. Work was one part of their lives, one element of who they were, but their identities were distinguishable from their positions. So was play. These women had developed an ability to detach from any single role and to move in and out of several roles relatively smoothly.

Women have traditionally carried multiple roles, gathering new ones without being willing or able to set down others. Consequently, women have been spouses and parents, caregivers to members of their families, volunteers at their children's schools, workers in and out of the home, constantly stitching each segment of their lives into the whole. Because women see their identities as a whole, however, their roles tend not to be compartmentalized. They are at work the same person they are at home. "I am a clergywoman; I am a single parent," one woman describes herself. Another explains, "I am late because my mother called and I needed to stop over at her house and make sure she was okay. I knew that you would understand that ministry includes family, so I was taking care of family."

Implications for the Small Church

The capacity to distinguish between various positions and roles—and to move in and out of them smoothly—is a definite advantage many women bring to ministry. Denominational officials, local congregations, and family members all have some expectations of what clergywomen in small churches will be and do. The ability to wear multiple and complex roles, while also being able to know what is needed at a particular time, is a useful skill for ministry. Being clear about our identity and the multiple roles we are living is central to our spiritual and emotional health.

Accepting and integrating our life experiences is also useful. Explains one clergywoman, "Previously I was a Southern Baptist; now I am a United Methodist. I served one congregation for nine years and was a director of Christian education for six years before coming to the two churches I now serve." This woman was able to integrate her broad experience in different denominations into her present identity as pastor of a small church. Her various roles are diverse: she had been married and is now single; she is a parent; she is a pastor, the first woman serving a church in the community, and the first female pastor the church has experienced. Taking such diversity and finding the common threads that unify and make whole is a challenging but important part of leadership in the small church.

Each church congregation has a unique, complex, and multifaceted identity as well. There is unity and strength in the identity of the small church. The geographical location (urban, rural, suburban) and the average size of worship attendance are a part of the church's identity. Likewise, the small church's identity is also very much a part of the fabric of the local culture. "We are who we are because of the history we carry. Our particular traditions and rituals help us to live out our cultural identity in a consistent way."[18] The history of the church in that community—whether the church is two hundred years old or less than one year—is an integral part of that church's identity.

The local community and the church community are linked by blood ties in leadership, history, and family connections: "Jim owns the funeral home in town and is the head trustee of the church. His father had the funeral home before him and was our head trustee." Some personal history gets stitched on the underside of the community because "they're one of us": "Donald had a bad first marriage. He moved away for a while and things didn't work out, so he's back here in town living up on Front Street and doing real well." The word *divorced* is never mentioned. It was a bad first marriage and things just didn't work out.

These and many other facets of the church's complex identity affect the expectations of clergy in ministry in the small church. Since the congregation has a complex array of items that together produce an identity, it is important to clarify expectations concerning who expects what from whom. The reality is that a church has an identity that is internal to its history; it also has an identity from the perspective and experience of the community, and the denomination may have a still different image of the church's identity. These three identities may be very different one from the other and they may be very different from the pastor's perception of the church's identity. Clarification of these multifaceted roles will be essential to offering leadership in that congregation.

These five qualities of leadership among women give us insight into the qualities needed for effective leadership in the small church. Each can make a significant contribution toward a pastor's leadership abilities in the small church. Conversely, each quality can be a detriment if ignored or devalued in the highly charged cultural setting of the small church. Many of these leadership qualities are transferable to larger congregations as well, but their impact is not felt as keenly. In the small church the leaders know one another and their families well. There is a common history and tradition that they have lived or have heard stories about all of their lives. The necessity for clergy to offer leadership that fits the setting, the people, and their vision is critical, though it is not an easy task. The complexities of small-church life are many, but fortunately there is no one way to be effective, no single route to success in ministry in the small church. Pastors need to make sense out of what they experience in their own lives. Pastors need to come as whole persons ready to be involved in sharing ministry, to affirm the uniqueness of the church and community, and ready to become a part of the congregation—its history and its future.

Questions for Reflection and Conversation

1. Sharing as a deliberate process
   a. When you look over the opportunities for sharing by the congregation, do you see any patterns in your church? Specifically, are the same persons sharing week after week, or is there a growing group of people who are comfortable sharing?
   b. If the congregation is a circle of leaders, with some being in the center and others scattered within the circle, where is your leadership located? What specific examples do you have of "reaching out" rather than "reaching down" in your congregation?
   c. What insights do you have on your own sharing as a deliberate process?

2. Paying attention to the larger context
   a. According to Tex Sample's categories of "cultural left," "cultural middle," and "cultural right," where do you place the members in your congregation? Where do you place yourself?
   b. What insights do you have about the language of the congregation and pulpit?

3. Being accessible
   a. Think back over the past week. List a number of unscheduled tasks and encounters, and ask yourself whether you considered each an interruption or not.
   b. Where is the grapevine of information in your church? Does the grapevine have a specific location, such as the local post office or in the parking lot after church? How do people spread news in the congregation? How did you learn about it, and who helped you?

4. Using pieces of time
   a. In the course of a typical day or week, approximately how many small breaks do you take?

    b. When you pace yourself, what do you do during your break times to increase your energy level? Name at least four ways of pacing that give you energy.

    c. What have you observed about the way the lay leaders in your church pace their energy?

5. Recognizing our complex and multifaceted identity

    a. What are the multiple roles that you have? What are the strengths and challenges you find in each of them?

Chapter 2

Caring For Your Spiritual Life

Ministry, the living out of God's call, is a constant challenge. Ministry is about relationships—and the small church calls forth every ounce of relational experience and insight available in its leaders, both lay and ordained.

The smaller the congregation or parish, the more intense is the need for relational skills. When the congregation consists of three families, all of whom have lived in the community all of their lives, the pastor is the outsider. Establishing a ministry among these folks takes no small effort. Any ministry in the church requires an attentiveness to the needs and concerns of other people, but ministry in the small church can make intense pastoral and relational demands on church leaders. In the midst of such challenges to give of ourselves in so many ways, it is critical that we be attentive to caring for our own spiritual lives while being attentive to the needs of others. In this chapter we will explore ways of doing just that.

Caring for one's own spiritual wholeness takes many different shapes and forms. Personal Bible study, prayer, and meditation are important avenues to nurture the spirit in daily living. Space away from the community for walking or learning is also a means of spiritual support for some leaders. "I walk four times a week," one pastor testifies. "That's a prayer time for me. My walk is around the loop. I pass the homes of my parishioners, and as I pass, I pray for my parishioners. We have a house not far away from the church. I often take one day a week and go there. That's where I do my sermon preparation. I also come to the seminary once a week."

Our spirituality is central to our identity and purpose, to remembering who we are, why we are here and how we are to be. Keeping one's spiritual life alive and whole is the centerpiece on the table of ministry, but the food on that table can sometimes be difficult to swallow. Conflicting needs and desires and inconsistencies between our experience and our sense of the way things ought to be contribute to the fragmentation of our spiritual lives.

The search for wholeness of spirit has been called the process of composition, "the activity of the human spirit seeking inner congruence with ultimate meanings."[1] When God calls and we respond, composition begins. Mary Catherine Bateson writes in her work *Composing a Life:* "I was constantly trying to make something coherent from conflicting elements to fit rapidly changing settings."[2]

We are living in a unique period of time in which women from various disciplines are finding their ways into new places of work. Their experiences, including those of Mary Catherine Bateson, remind us of the continuity of women's life experiences that intersect with specific places for ministry in the church. We are talking about living in a way that has credibility and meaning regardless of where we live. In the midst of much that is changing in the world, today's spiritual search becomes one of seeking integration rather than separation and division in living. In many situations, women in ministry have effectively modeled this notion of integration. Ministry in the small church usually means that you are your own secretary, custodian, and spiritual leader. The smaller the church, the more transparent the living.

When we tell stories that are central to our lives, we are unfolding our lived spirituality. The struggle in the journey to wholeness is the search for a consistency in our lives, a congruency between who we see ourselves to be—our self-image—and who we are called by God to be, a consistency between the values we say are important to us and the decisions we actually make. Each decision is stitched to a value we hold. Each part of the search for spirituality is about having an integrity about our living and believing that we are earnestly seeking God's direction in our life.

The search for a wholeness of spirit is fluid: it has movement, rather than being static. Often when we come to a plateau in that journey we have a sense of being stopped: things seem to be the same, beyond the point of being interesting any longer. Rather than being stumbling blocks in our way, these moments can be occasions of our becoming aware that there are probably other ways we can grow in our spiritual lives, and if we are willing to try them we can begin a new leg of the journey.

The movement of this journey is also cyclical rather than lin-ear. Three themes, based on the metaphor of the journey as composition, can be useful in helping us understand some of the ways we can attend to our spiritual lives: identifying discordant notes, beginning the process of improvisation, and living the composition.

Theme One: Identifying Discordant Notes

The dictionary defines discordant notes as notes that are har-monically unresolved, that are marked by dissonance, clashing, a lack of agreement. The "discordant notes" of our spirituality are the inconsistencies between the beliefs we hold, and be-tween our actions and our beliefs. The question then is, how do we learn to "hear" the discordant notes in our lives, the incon sistencies that raise issues of great concern to us?

Spiritually discordant notes are heard most clearly in periods of transitions, both transitions by choice and those transitions that are thrust upon us by circumstances beyond our control. For example, some middle-aged clergy tell of the struggle of hearing God's call to enter full-time ministry while they were still in the midst of other kinds of work. Their struggle to respond to God's call involved finding ways to reconcile the demands of ministry with their present responsibilities.

Cultural transitions are also often the place in which we hear the discordant notes of inconsistencies between what we believe and the values we hold, and what we see around us. The per-sonal, highly relational values of the small church, for example, are being challenged at every corner. Now we bank with a card in a machine on the outside of buildings instead of speaking with a human being. We can call for pizza in a video store. We can teach and learn by satellite. People move frequently, and families are configured in new ways as divorce and remarriage becomes more common. The cultural continuity previous gener-ations depended on is not available today.

Charles Handy, in his book *The Age of Unreason,* suggests that the discontinuities we experience today make this a time of "un-reason." What we once reasonably expected to take place in our lives probably will not now. Careers are no longer for a lifetime. More adults are leaving full-time employment in their late forties and early fifties.[3] Studies show that middle-aged adults are will-ing to sell their talent, but not all their time. These adults are redefining the sacred cultural cows of work and leisure.

Handy also notes that even *where* we perform those careers is

changing: "By some estimates, one-quarter of the working pop-
ulation will be working from home by the end of this century.
From home is different from at home. The home is the base not
the prison. We can leave it. . . . By taking the job, physically,
outside the organization, we make it more our own."[4] The way
in which we work from home has also changed. A decade ago
when people worked at home they stayed at home, with a
phone, a computer, and maybe a copier machine. Today we
leave our "from home" work spaces through the fax, the phone
with its answering service and capability for conference calls,
and portable computers with modems. (It is perhaps interesting
to note that persons in ministry in the small church have being
working in "from home" work spaces for years.) As incremental
changes, sometimes only barely recognizable, occur within the
culture, the weight of their combined impact significantly affects
our future and makes us aware of discontinuities and inconsistencies in our experience. We can no longer act as if nothing has
changed.

The church has also known the discordant notes of transition
between what it was and what it is called to become. The questions "Who are we?" and "Why are we?" are disquieting, but
these and other questions become the catalysts for change, the
keys that unlock new spaces to be explored. However, change
involves leaving the known, safe, secure religious world we created. Seminaries across the country are full of women students
who are experiencing the effects of discontinuous change. Their
very presence has also produced a discontinuity in seminary life
as we have known it.

In the midst of such turmoil and change, even in the church,
how can we find the wholeness of spirit we seek? Sharon Parks
compares spiritual turmoil to the effects of a shipwreck: "Shipwreck is the coming apart of what has served as shelter and pro-
tection and has held and carried one where one wanted to
go—the collapse of a structure that once promised trustworthi-
ness. . . . when we undergo the shipwreck of meaning at the
level of faith, we feel threatened at the very core of our existence."[5] These shipwrecks can be any crisis that threatens our
confidence and security, such as the loss of a job or a divorce.

Carl Jung's work refers to a similar experience, but he uses the
image of a "night sea journey," the times of crises when transitions are made. "For Jung, the part of life which is essential is
not the biographical part but the myth, the 'spiritual inner side
of this life.' "[6] Transitions through night sea journeys or during
times of shipwreck are times of crisis and change in our lives. At

these times some of us become immobilized rather than energized, refusing or unable to make decisions that would help us
move through the crisis. We can spend many hours in night sea
journeys or being shipwrecked, choosing to stop our inner spiritual journey at such transitions by longing for the old, familiar
ways, wallowing in ministry without a sense of direction. In
such instances, the locus of authority has been allowed to reside
outside of rather than within the individual; personal choice is
given away to the will and expectations of others. Yet transitions
and crises can also offer us an open space where we are free to
take the pieces of spirituality and make a new composition, free
to answer the "who are we?" and "why are we?" questions, free
to create a fresh relationship with God.

But we know that moving into the unknown, leaving the safe,
secure world we have known, means encountering unfamiliar
circumstances. Until the point of the threshold or exit is reached
and crossed, there remains in one's ears the discordant notes,
the dissonant sounds of discontinuity.

Theme Two: Improvising Our Song

Improvisation is the art of making, inventing, and rearranging
what we make. When we risk continuity (the way life has always
been) to respond to chords of discontinuity (the way life could
be), we begin to improvise. Improvisation is not created from
nothing; instead, it calls forth all our past experiences and wisdom. To improvise is to create anew from what is old, to begin to
weave the silken threads of past satisfactions into an emerging
pattern.

What helps us to improvise? In *Composing a Life,* Mary
Catherine Bateson reminds us that the process of remembering
is a rich well from which to draw our strength. Sometimes we
find ourselves whistling or humming the melody of a tune until
the words come. Putting words to past experiences, remembering past times that remind us of present ones help us to find
some continuity within this new composition. We must remember that we have in fact composed before. And we have the resources both to create new compositions and to improvise on the
ones we have already composed.

One resource for our improvisation is *play.* Ministry is serious
and time-consuming work, and often what gets crowded out of a
busy week is time to play. A part of spiritual wholeness is remembering that play is essential to keeping spiritual life alive.

Gerhard Wehr tells a delightful story about Carl Jung. When

he was in his mid-thirties and was groping after the structures of the collective unconscious, he yielded to his inner impulse to play as he did when he was a boy of ten or eleven. Carl Jung "collected little stones on the shore of Lake Zurich and began playfully building a whole village; a village with a church and finally also—after some hesitation—an altar." Jung recalled, "Naturally, I thought about the significance of what I was doing, and asked myself, 'Now, really, what are you about? You are building a small town, and doing it as if it were a rite!' I had no answer to my question, only the inner certainty that I was on the way to discovering my own myth. For the building game was only a beginning."⁷ Through play Jung came to a turning point where he moved from a sense of complete helplessness to an inward calm for reweaving his life.

Church leaders can also rework their lives through play. Allowing time for play in the midst of much that is serious and scheduled in their ministries can help to combat inner stagnation, and can bring fresh sounds to the monotone of their spiritual lives.

Playing hard brings new wounds, but deep wounds and old scars have the capacity to teach us. We all carry scars that remind us of how harsh life can be, and sometimes during improvisation we are hurt. *Watching for new teachers* is a second resource we can draw on in our compositions. Robert Bly has noted, "Some old traditions say that no man is adult until he has become opened to the soul and spirit world, and they say that such an opening is done by a wound in the right place, at the right time, in the right company. A wound allows the spirit or soul to enter."⁸ I believe this wounding into adulthood is equally true for women.

I have a friend who says that when he was young, his teachers had faces and names. They were real people complete with addresses and zip codes. Now, in adulthood, his teachers are pains in the body that won't stop, relationships that are broken, disputes that must be settled with others.⁹ Our wounds can reveal to us our places of vulnerability, and *accessing our places of vulnerability* is another resource for improvisation. Bateson suggests that two places of vulnerability can stifle spiritual and personal growth: self-sacrifice that sets self-interests aside to be used or misused by others, and distorting the vision of self.¹⁰

When we think about improvisation, we imagine how things could be, we take another look at how we want to be. Improvisation does not usually come easily on the first try. But teachers are all around us, and if we watch for them we can learn from their wisdom and experience, and incorporate what they have to teach us into our spiritual lives.

Theme Three: Living Out the Composition

The compositions of our lives are the result of a long process of arranging, mixing, and combining various ingredients into a complex, artistic form. They are the measure of congruency between who we say we are and who we really are, the credibility check of inner integrity with outer living. Living life as a composition means we "live it out on our feet."

One Mother Superior, in addressing her community, compared church ministry and leadership to breadmaking: "The task of administration in the business of breadmaking would be to see that the congregational budget includes the funds necessary to buy the flour, yeast, sugar; to purchase all the necessary ingredients and to be sure the oven works. It is the task of leadership to plunge its hands into the dough, to feel the life within it, to serve that life by kneading, baking, and offering it as nourishment. In a very real sense 'we' are not making the bread . . . the bread is making itself."[11]

In the image of breadmaking this woman finds congruency between her inner life and her outer leadership in the congregation. As she kneads the bread, she is aware of the life within the bread itself. Likewise, our challenge is to feel, see, know, and respond to the inner life and how it connects to what we are doing. The basic ingredients represent the starting point from which we begin to work. The ingredients, the way we blend them, and the baker are all to be considered. We are all breadmakers. We are challenged to mix ingredients and to create that which will be nourishing and will sustain life. Once the resources we have for improvisation are identified, the composing can begin.

We compose and arrange for the purpose of living out the harmony within. How can persons in ministry live the composition? The nature of an improvised composition is that it is unlike what we have seen and heard before, even though the ingredients may be familiar. Learning to live with ambiguity and to create new ways to work the ingredients can be difficult and frustrating.

"In fact, we all talk . . . as if it [our life] were a flower bed continually invaded by wild flowers that we are all reluctant to pull out. Our days are reminiscent of Edna St. Vincent Millay's "Por-

trait by a Neighbour": "Even when we try to be more disci-
plined: 'Her lawn looks like a meadow,/And if she mows the
place/She leaves the clover standing/And the Queen Anne's
lace!' "[12] Spirituality begins at the place in the flower bed where
the wild flowers appear and are permitted to remain.

Living the composition of our spiritual lives is about living
through discontinuities and living with ambiguities. It is about
entering "new space" by choice or not by choice, following instead of leading, hearing instead of speaking, learning instead of
preaching. This kind of living involves taking a fresh look at our
new teachers and at our experience. And, finally, it means being
present to God.

The Cycle of Spirituality

These three themes make it clear that the inner journey to spiritual wholeness is cyclical in nature. In our search for meaning in
life we may enter this circle at any place. If we enter the circle
with discontinuity, for example, we are seeking some kind of
change in our living. We have energy to examine our relationship
to God and others and perhaps the way we are living out our
values. The restlessness and discontent we feel in our present
lives draw us to begin the search of what could be.

Moving through the initial phase of rethinking and imaging
what is carries us into a time for improvisation. During this
phase we begin to reweave threads from our past. Experiences
that may have seemed like separate threads on the fringes of our
lives are now gathered and brought into the main pattern, accepted and integrated as part of who we are. In improvisation we
search for ways to take our past history, positive and negative,
and to let it teach us, gaining strength and courage from it. This
phase is perhaps the most difficult because we are without maps
to guide us: uncharted ground must be walked a step at a time,
and unfamiliar ground may be painful for our feet. Those who
have experience with walking in new spaces often provide encouragement to new travelers. They are the wisdom-keepers
who tell new travelers stories of how they struggled, and how
they kept courage for the journey.

Our spiritual search is for a composition of life that has a continuity between who we see ourselves to be and who we really are
as we live out our values and beliefs day by day. We seek consistency in our lives. As we move through the cycle of spirituality,
we stretch to understand who God is in our lives and how we

Cycle of Spirituality

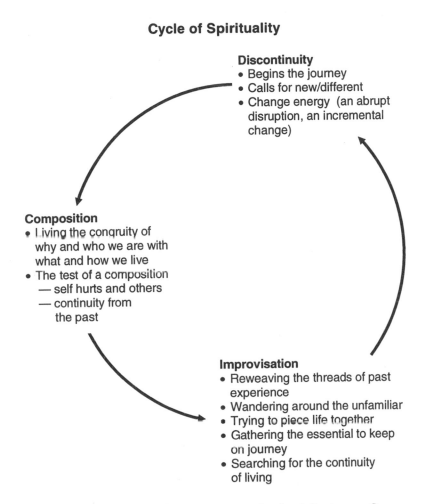

Discontinuity
- Begins the journey
- Calls for new/different
- Change energy (an abrupt disruption, an incremental change)

Composition
- Living the congruity of why and who we are with what and how we live
- The test of a composition
  — self hurts and others
  — continuity from the past

Improvisation
- Reweaving the threads of past experience
- Wandering around the unfamiliar
- Trying to piece life together
- Gathering the essential to keep on journey
- Searching for the continuity of living

may use the gifts God has given to us in the fullest way. Once a new composition is reached we often find ourselves being tugged and pulled once again into discontinuity. New ways of responding to God emerge and we begin a new journey.

God's call is constant. The destination is not what gives us energy: the energy is for the journey, the search to be the person God has given us gifts to be.

Questions for Reflection and Conversation

1. How would you describe your spiritual life at this point in time? Is it thriving? satisfying? stagnant? dying? nonexistent?

2. What discontinuities around you are directly affecting your spiritual health?

3. Of the discontinuities you listed, which do you have the potential to affect or alter in some positive way? How can you be a catalyst for change?

4. Can you identify what is missing in your relationship with God? What would improve your relationship with God?

5. How does play help you to keep your spiritual balance?

6. Who are your new teachers, and what are you learning about your spiritual life?

Chapter 3

Rituals
That Grace Ministry

"There are always fresh flowers from the field on the altar. When we come to the Communion table, we know that Harriett has baked the bread and her husband has made the wooden cutting board so that each piece is the same size," relates one small-church pastor.

"When a baby is born in our congregation," says another, "there is always a fresh rose on the altar."

Rituals such as these emerge out of a church's character and history. We are continually in the process of creating new ones and tenaciously holding on to those that have always been a part of who we are. In this chapter we will define the nature and role of rituals and explore how people in leadership in small churches create, encourage, and participate in rituals.

What Are Rituals?

Rituals are patterned, predictable, repetitive behaviors that can be either formal or informal. They are often subtle, natural movements and patterns that emerge over time. Rituals are part of the fabric of our lives, and of the small church.

The oral historians in the congregation can tell you when and how different rituals in the church and community originated. Over breakfast one day, for instance, a lay leader revealed to the pastor a bit of personal and church history: "Do you know who was first involved in getting the Easter service moved to Mrs. Clark's home? I was." The smile on the pastor's face conveyed to this oral historian that she had received and welcomed another piece of the church's historical quilt.

In the small church, ritual is often birthed around major events such as Easter, Christmas, and community celebrations. Knowing how the congregation came to particular rituals and who participated in their creation gives church leaders insight into how other changes might occur in the future. Each ritual is related to a larger tradition and ways of doing things.

Certain objects, equipment, and techniques can assist us in our rituals. Rituals can be physical, mental, seasonal, historical, and playful.[1] A lunch for the family following a funeral is an example of a *physical ritual. Mental rituals* include the informal ways in which we welcome new members and know when to begin a meeting or service. Advent and Lent are times for *seasonal rituals,* which for some congregations include a breakfast with sausage and biscuits or a weekday Lenten meal. *Historical rituals* include how a congregation tells its story. Our church celebrated the centennial by making six needlepoint medallions that now hang on the social room wall. Each medallion tells a part of the history of our congregation. *Playful rituals* include basketball or softball leagues, picnics for the whole congregation, potluck suppers, and talent nights.

Each ritual has a critical place and performs a specific function in the life of the small church. William Willimon and Robert Wilson have identified five such functions: rituals confirm the identity of a group, link us with our past, help us to create community, assist us in maintaining corporate values and norms, and provide support for coping with stress and anxiety.[2]

Identifying and keeping track of these rituals and their significance in the church is a challenge for any pastor. When church leaders consider the meaning of a particular ritual in the life of their congregation, they need to ask questions like, "What does the ritual do for the social life or community solidarity?" "How does ritual fit in the structure and shape of the faith community?" "How does the ritual cause a change or awakening in the participant's emotions?" and "What is the origin of this ritual and who perpetuates it?"[3] The answers to these and other questions can help clergy and other church leaders to understand the significance and role of rituals in the church community.

Characteristics of Rituals

A number of liturgists, sociologists, theologians, and church leaders have reflected and written on the characteristics of rituals. Their work provides valuable insights concerning the place of rituals in the life of the small church. I would like to focus on five characteristics of rituals that are particularly significant in the small church. They are:

1. Rituals are repetitive acts.
2. Rituals are sacred and profane, positive and negative.
3. Rituals have an aspect of obligation.
4. Rituals provide a relatively reliable index of family integration.
5. Rituals have something of the eternal.

1. Rituals are repetitive acts.

We call getting up in the morning and following a particular set routine our "morning ritual." It might include brushing our teeth, taking a shower, dressing, having a Bible study and prayer time. We do the same acts each morning, often in the same order.

Rituals are repetitive by definition. Rituals "act out and sacralize sameness. They maximize order by strengthening the place of the individual in the group, or society, and vice versa by strengthening the bonds of a society *vis-à-vis* the individual. They unify, integrate, and sacralize."[4]

At one church, the ushers always go outside on the church steps after collecting the offering. At another, it is understood that you "don't go in the kitchen unless you ask Hilda; she doesn't take kindly to people moving her pots and pans." Places like church steps and kitchens may hold years of ritual history of which we are unaware unless we are told. The ritual keepers are usually persons who have been members for a long time and have claimed spaces as their own. Within the space of the ushers and the kitchen keepers, rituals have developed concerning what you do when you are in these spaces.

2. Rituals are sacred and profane, positive and negative.

Rituals are not confined to religious organizations. A Sunday afternoon walk or a particular way we come to the dinner table can also involve ritual. According to author W. S. F. Pickering, "Whereas negative rites separate the spheres of the sacred and the profane, and bring home to the worshiper the nature and total undesirability of the profane, positive rites directly introduce him [or her] to the sacred."[5] For example, a negative rite would be not eating certain foods during Lent. This negative rite would "ensure the continued status of the sacred."[6]

The two central functions of positive rites are recall and euphoria. According to sociologist Emile Durkheim, "Rites have a profound effect on the participants, not only individually but as a group, and not only intellectually but emotionally."[7] He goes on to suggest that often participants cannot clearly see the real impact of rites at the moment. The full value of the experience is only seen later, after sufficient time has elapsed and the individual begins the process of recalling the event. Recalling the ceremony or ritual awakens "certain ideas and sentiments, to attach the present to the past, or the individual to the group."[8]

When parishioner Rebecca Hildreth returned from the university to her home church for her wedding, the ceremony was itself a ritual of recall. The small church was bulging with folding chairs so that everyone who was part of her growing up could come. Becky wore her mother-in-law's wedding dress, which linked the "new family" with her own. The story spread pew to pew before Becky walked down the aisle: "The wedding dress belongs to Mrs. Wade, and Becky is the fourth bride to wear the dress."

The other function of positive rituals, euphoria, refers to what happens when we gather together. We do not experience the same emotions individually that we do when we hear the sound of others' voices, see familiar faces, and experience the warmth of particular words. There is a common reservoir of life that sustains us in a way that being alone cannot.

Tory's family knew the importance of rituals that sustain. Tory was just a few days old when she died, and our gathering for the burial service was a sad experience for her family and their friends. The words spoken, the familiar faces, though filled with pain, the ritual of standing in a circle for prayer, were our only comfort in such a tragic time. It was a service in which ritual comforted and transported us into the next hour. We called on the common reservoir of life to sustain us.

The service to celebrate Tory's life was also a service of recall. Each person was challenged to remember sources of strength and comfort during other dark moments of life. Recalling times of tragedy and despair brought back the memory of working with other losses. As an extended family, we sang hymns and listened to Scripture and the homily. We reminded one another that no one was alone in grief. Our past experiences with grief, individually and collectively, became reservoirs of strength and courage.

The intent of ritual is, as Durkheim argues, "to take the audience away from the real world and to transport them into another which is readily open to the imagination."[9] In the example of Tory's funeral, the service was the constant, the calm in an uncontrollable circumstance.

3. Rituals have an aspect of obligation.

We receive from God; we give back to God. The characteristic of obligation is about the relationship that is formed by an exchange of services. We are recipients of God's gifts, and we are obliged to give in return to God. The Bible calls us to give the first fruits of our labor. Prayers of thanksgiving offer our gratitude to God.

Traditional Thanksgiving services are examples of rituals of obligation. Another example would be when all the churches in the Johnstown area gathered after the flood in a service of thanksgiving. Still another would be the story of a religious community of two hundred Roman Catholic sisters celebrating Mass. As the Mother Superior dipped a fresh tree branch in a basin of water and as the choir sang, she walked and sprinkled members with the water—drops of blessing, an offering of thanksgiving for each life and each contribution to the community. Receiving the drops of water reminded each sister that she is blessed and loved by God. When, in the Old Testament story, Hannah took her son Samuel to Eli, she dedicated—gave back to God—the child God had given to her. Persons who make vows at confirmations, weddings, or services of consecration, dedication, or ordination are promising to remember their obligation to God and God's people.

As a diaconal minister in the United Methodist Church, I am reminded that God has given first. As the recipient of God's gifts, I am obligated to receive them, give thanks for them, and return them to God in some way. Although this is not an obligation in the sense in which our culture uses the word, it is an act of joyful gratitude.

The greatest pitfall is that weekly worship would lull us into obligation in ritual in such a way that the thanksgiving would be rote rather than real and challenging. At their best, rituals can freshen worship, can help us to remember and be renewed. Rituals return us to our experiences, prompt us to recall, and remind us of the Giver.

4. Rituals provide a relatively reliable index of family integration.

It is often through observing rituals that we come to understand the health and wholeness of the church family.

Do they pass the peace every Sunday? Is the congregation

friendly? Do they fight with one another? Are they always in turmoil over something?

According to author Barbara Hargrove, "There is a universal tendency for religion to become ritualized, to involve highly predictable patterns of behavior and words. . . . In those areas of life where it is most difficult to predict what is going to happen next or what can be done about it, we can in reaction so rigidly structure our behavior that every detail is predictable."[10] Knowing that rigidity may be a part of those stress-filled times at least sheds some light on the insanity of minutia for some. Babies crying and people coming into the pews long after the service has started may not be an issue ninety percent of the time. But when there is a strain on the congregation, these "every Sunday occurrences" may take on a new level of irritation. During times of stress or crisis, the concept of "reaction formation" may take over the congregation.

Similarly, if a new pastor tries to change the order of worship, the congregation may react with hostility. This reaction is more likely if the family, church, or home comes together at mealtime only infrequently, and the family is a scattered, less-than-cohesive unit. On the other hand, when problems, issues, and concerns are brought to the table rather than to the parking lot and private conversations, there is a high probability that the family is valuing life together, and expressing that life through the rituals they keep.

5. "There is something of the eternal in ritual."

Carl Jung believed that "ritual restored wholeness," and Erik Erikson spoke of how "faith can serve as a 'ritual restoration of a sense of trust.' "[11] According to Leonel Mitchell, "Ultimately the meaning of ritual is festivity, the celebration of redeemed creation and ourselves as a part of it. It is a participation in the Divine life, and a sharing in its love."[12]

When we sing, cry, hear special music, or dance, we taste of the eternal. Hearing the choir sing as they process down the center aisle of a small church, feeling the walls shake with the power of their voices, feeling a beat and a rhythm that speaks to the soul in a special way—all confirm once again that we are more than voice and actions. When rituals relate us to the eternal, we are indeed ritual-rich.

Durkheim asserted, "Rituals are not aberrations; there are profound reasons for them in the very nature of things, . . . there is something of the eternal in ritual."[13] For Durkheim, there is indeed something beyond the immediate with which we connect when we participate in ritual. For Jung, individuation, or the wholeness of living, comes to the fore with ritual. "Ritual," says Hans J. Mol, "also restores identity, particularly when disruption has occurred, for example, through death, or when rearrangements in marriage or family relations become necessary."[14]

When Judy's divorce became final, she asked her pastor for a service of wholeness. Judy's identity had always been linked to the church. She was baptized, confirmed, and married in the church. She took promises and covenants seriously, and her divorce was a shattering of expectations. She needed the church's support and confirmation of her new singleness. Asking that the pastor, her family, and a few friends gather to bless her new life and her wholeness was a ritual about her identity as a person striving to be faithful to God and the church. The service was a ritual of restoration.

Identifying with a sense of the eternal gives individuals the continuity necessary to carry on with their lives, often in ways and directions they themselves might not have chosen. Saying that ritual aids us in touching the eternal is to remind us of the importance of the familiar, the routine, those simple acts of ritual that connect us with tradition and history. Our identity, our wholeness, our need to connect with that which is eternal, is often fulfilled through ritual. The remembering of the eternal in ritual has restorative power. In the small church, rituals offer both the recall of tradition and the euphoria of repetitive patterns.

Ten Silent Rituals

The two most important and visible rituals of the church are Communion and baptism. These and other visible rituals help newcomers to see "the way we do it here." But there are also less visible rituals that are an important part of the life of the church. I call these rituals "silent rituals" because they are seldom discussed. They emerge in a congregation over the years and are reenacted each time the congregation comes together. Often these small acts are overlooked or go unnoticed. Yet each has the power and potential to inform church leaders of the ways a particular faith community lives out and renews its identity.

Silent rituals combine traditional rituals of the wider church with local rituals, and are unique for each person, congregation, and pastor. A congregation creates and adapts its own version of these rituals. The challenge of silent rituals is in the complicated layering of the moment and the delicacy of living and participating as pastors in the midst of these rituals. Emile Durkheim reminds us that "Hidden in ritual is a reality of greatest significance."[15] Rituals have the power to persist through changes, and have a quality of universality that transcends individual congregations.[16] But church leaders need to be aware of the local variations on silent rituals in their congregation. A seminarian told the following story: "The leaders didn't understand why I wanted a key to the church. They told me: 'When you need to get into the church . . . call Mr. Phillips and he will come and unlock the door for you.' " The ritual of key keeping was set, and all pastors before had abided by the ritual of "getting the doors unlocked."

I have heard many clergywomen tell stories about the silent rituals in their congregations. They usually encourage the use of rituals, and enjoy participating in the creation of new rituals. Women are often particularly attentive to these rituals. Clergymen, too, understand and encourage silent rituals; however, clergywomen may see these more quickly and understand them without much explanation. The world of silence that women have known for so long seems to be an advantage in seeing, encouraging, and creating these rituals.

From the stories I have heard and the studies I have undertaken concerning the role and nature of rituals in the small church, I have identified ten silent rituals that provide a way to understand the importance of rituals and ministry-enhancing ways of participating in rituals. All ten are about understanding the unwritten dynamics of the small church, its people and place. To my knowledge, there are no seminary courses that alert pastors to the existence of these rituals. Yet each silent ritual is extremely powerful in shaping a faith community.

The ten silent rituals I have identified are:

1. Rituals within a ritual
2. Baptism
3. Easter
4. Make a home
5. Adoption
6. Naming
7. Counting faces
8. Waiting and beginning
9. Space
10. Place

The first three are about the layering and complexity of seeing and understanding ritual within the small church. Both baptism and Easter sunrise show how local faith community rituals grow around major, traditional rituals. Rituals four through eight are about how a pastor and congregation come together, begin their living, and accept one another. The last two are about location and ritual.

1. Rituals within a ritual

The funeral itself is a ritual; the funeral dinner is the silent ritual developed within the funeral ritual. The caring, support, and personal attentiveness to feeding and strengthening during the time of crisis is enhanced by this meal. Individual congregations will develop distinctive ways of performing this ritual within a ritual. At Bellflower Church, people come back to see the flowers in the Bellflower cemetery. The church's pastor, Evelyn, tells of the unique Bellflower Church funeral dinner ministry: "We have only eight in our group, and two of those are unable to function as helpers in the kitchen. We have many people who come back to Bellflower to be buried. We have a beautiful cemetery, and people come to it over Memorial Day to see the flowers. I have had many funerals because the people grew up in our church; they have come back now, and the women put on the funeral dinner for them."

In this case, the rituals within a ritual include both the meal and the coming back to see the flowers. These traditions are an example of how silent rituals become part of a more formal ritual in a given community. A pastor's encouragement and appreciation for the history of this complex ritual is central to knowing and understanding this congregation.

2. Baptism

When Evelyn, a pastor, tells the story of Jake's baptism, we hear two rituals: one of the baptism itself and one that recounts how she became woven into the history of the congregation. "We've watched Jake grow from the three-week-old infant whom I baptized on Mother's Day. It was really a touching experience for me. Jake was the first baby I baptized. Now he is a toddler." Baptizing or dedicating persons is an act of welcoming into the community. Evelyn was in on the beginning of Jake's life in this congregation. They could mark the passing of time in their lives together. And because Evelyn was already a part of the congregational community welcoming Jake, this ritual actually marked at least two occasions: Jake's entrance and Evelyn's participation in welcoming. The silent ritual of welcoming was an integral part of the ritual of baptism.

One congregation has a welcoming ritual where the pastor holds the newborn and walks into the congregation. Songs are sung using the baby's and the parents' names. Then the oldest member of the congregation is called out of the pew and lays hands on the infant. The newborn is touched by the generations, traditions, and the history of the faith community. In this ritual one who knows little is touched by one who knows much, bringing together yesterday, today, and tomorrow.

3. Easter

Although the celebration of Easter is a major ritual in most churches, unique traditions will emerge. Particular routines carry meaning and are central to understanding how a congregation participates in a major Christian ritual such as Easter.

Easter rituals in congregations focus on how we gather and what we do when we gather. One pastor described the Easter ritual as a time when the family comes together for breakfast: "We serve sausage and biscuits to as many as we can hold—and then some." The family will be fed both physically and spiritually.

There is a silent ritual within this ritual: the complex movement of people with multiple responsibilities. In one church the organist was also the organizer in the kitchen. Music is important in the small church, but when the Easter breakfast comes, a high-school-age substitute plays the organ so the meal for the church family can be prepared. This particular story tells a great deal about organizational structure in the small church, where multiple roles emerge once again.

An Easter sunrise service on Mrs. Thelma Parker's lawn is a tradition in the Sheffield Church. Mrs. Parker's home is located on the mill pond, which is the distinctive attraction of the community and the county. Her gazebo and lawn are a lovely setting for the service. The lawn goes right up to the water, and Spanish moss hangs gracefully on the tree branches. Mrs. Parker is house-bound, and the sunrise service is an opportunity for her to be with the congregation and friends in the community. Easter sunrise service on Mrs. Parker's lawn has become a ritual within a ritual in that congregation.

In these and countless other ways that will be unique to each congregation, the major ritual of Easter is surrounded by silent rituals of place, caretaking, and hospitality.

4. To make home

Ministry in the small church is about how the pastor and the congregation minister together. For new pastors especially, being welcomed and knowing how to receive welcome is important, and will indicate how the congregation will receive newcomers to the church. What are the rituals of welcoming that we receive and that we offer? Understanding how "to make home" is about knowing ways to welcome. The struggle for the new pastor is that she or he comes into the church last, while members of the church family are already in their home space.

Sometimes a new pastor offers an open house so that folks can walk through the space and receive the gift of hospitality from the pastor. Other times the congregation holds the reception. Whatever ritual of welcoming the church has, pastors will find themselves in that awkward place of having to figure out how to participate. It is difficult for some clergy to let themselves be known. Some of this awkwardness is knowing how to move from guest to host. Guests wait until they are greeted, but hosts move around and welcome.

Sometimes congregations are the ones to struggle with how to offer to and receive welcome from their new pastor. When Pastor Sharon set her chairs on the front porch of the parsonage, some folks came by and told her, "Don't get too comfortable. Pastors don't last long here." Ministry in the small church is relational and contextual and needs people and place, and no pastor can be in ministry alone, without the support and welcome of the congregation. The silent rituals of welcoming and "making home" are critical to beginning a ministry together.

5. Adoption

Adoption or acceptance is a rite of initiation into the church family. A pastor can be welcomed to a church and can serve a church without being adopted. There is no forced adoption in the small church! The congregation probably has existed over the years despite mediocre leadership, excellent leadership, or no leadership at all. They will not be hurried or bullied into adopting pastors. The pace of the adoption process is up to the leadership of the congregation, as they respond to the new pastor.

Rites of initiation include those rituals that celebrate rebirth and resurrection. Being adopted by a congregation is about being born into a new family. Author Mircea Eliade says, "The ceremony entitles the individual to participate in the life of the 'spirit' or 'culture,' a privilege which does not belong to those who have not undergone it. Initiation, therefore, involves both the processes of death and birth, return to chaos. . . . The initiate is ritually killed and then brought into being again."[17]

Congregations either adopt pastors or choose to live with them but not adopt them, just as they choose or do not choose to adopt members. Joining a church or being called or appointed to a congregation does not ensure adoption. Although there are some commonalities, each congregation has its own process of adoption. Rituals are a part of the adoption process. Each repetitive behavior is a hint at the historical story that has woven the present together with the past. Every ritual tells a story. Each new ritual is weaving in a significant new story that will be retold as part of the adoption process.

While Joanne was completing her seminary studies she also served a church. When she moved to the Valencia Church, she let it be known that her commitment was for six years, not just for her years in seminary. "In some ways that was selfish, because I knew that in six years my daughter would graduate from high school in the same area. But I didn't want the church to feel that once I finished seminary I was gone." When the congregation knows that a pastor is planning to stay for a while, a more stable environment for ministry is created.

Joanne's adoption by the congregation came slowly, over time. Shortly after she arrived, a prominent member of the church died. Because of the way she was present with the family, both for the funeral and following the funeral, Joanne could feel the warmth and the acceptance of major leaders in the church family. Another part of Joanne's adoption process occurred two and a half years later, when she came upon a car just overturned on the highway. Recognizing the vehicle to be one owned by a parishioner, Sue, Pastor Joanne stopped to help. To this day, Sue often remarks, "I still can't get over the day Joanne showed up when I had my accident." Joanne was also the one who called Sue's daughter to tell her of the accident. Through these and other significant events in the life of the congregation, Joanne experienced the silent ritual of adoption by the congregation.

The pastoral presence during difficult times of crisis, grieving, and celebrating in the lives of church members is critical to the adoption process. Pastors may become part of the inner family at these times, and the normally slow adoption process may be accelerated. Critical moments in the life of the congregation, such as accidents, deaths, marriages, and baptisms, are natural times for a congregation to silently consider the "adoptability" of the pastor through seeing how the pastor relates to people in these moments.

There are few signs and guideposts to give direction to the new pastor. Adoption is about changing one's place in the community. This is a participatory process, and the one who is being adopted is not able to accelerate the process. By contrast, ordination has a sequence of predictable steps. When pastors are ordained, the ceremony is a ritual of initiation into a new role. Although ordination and adoption are both rites of initiation, adoption involves much more uncharted territory.

Adoption rituals in the church can also be intertwined with adoption rituals by the community. Susan, a pastor serving two rural churches, tells her story of conversations at the Chicken House restaurant. She explains: "The Chicken House is the center of the social scene in the town. There is a women's table and a men's table. All the local issues are discussed and local news transmitted around these tables." Susan's being invited by a woman to come to the Chicken House and sit at the table was an indication of her step-by-step adoption by the community. To be "at table" is to be trusted with conversation.

The Chicken House is where the grapevine operates for the Valley Chapel Church. For Susan's other church, the Sugar Creek Church, the grapevine is in the Sunday school hour and in the women's meeting. Learning where people gather for conversation and being included in those gatherings is part of the adoption process. Other places where folks might gather to tell stories include post offices, gas stations, barbershops, and grocery stores.

Adoption is optional, and the congregation decides whether or not they wish to adopt the pastor. A denomination may appoint or a committee may call a pastor, but only the leaders in the small-church congregation will decide if the pastor is to be adopted. It is not possible to create a forced adoption between the central offices and the small church or between the pastor and the small church. Once the church doors are closed, the local leaders will decide whom they will and will not accept.

Certain leaders are pivotal in the adoption process. These persons may include the matriarch and/or patriarch and the doorkeeper. These designated persons informally "tell the history in story" to the pastor. How a pastor receives these informal story hours affects the next step of the adoption process. Pastors who are not cultural historians and who do not care to hear the stories are seldom, if ever, adopted.

The time an adoption takes can vary from weeks to years. Since the critical times for a congregation are unpredictable, it is difficult to know when the adoption process will be accelerated. Crises accelerate the conversation on adoption; a pastor's inability to appreciate the "stories" can slow the process down.

Other silent rituals intertwine with the ritual of adoption. No ritual stands alone. Naming and welcoming are important in the adoption process. There may be a sequence of welcoming, making home, and naming which precede the actual adoption.

6. The ritual of naming

The small church is a primary group. One of the basic characteristics of a primary group is that it encourages the characters of its members to emerge. The best example we have of a primary group is a family. As families name and give nicknames to their members—Runt, Shortie, Padre, Little Red—so a church names its characters. In one church there was a woman whom everyone called "Mrs." No one ever used any other name for her. Her son was called Spider. Jesus called his disciples James, John, Andrew, Judas. Jesus did not refer to them as "the twelve disciples" but as individuals. The disciples sat at meal together, fished on the Sea of Galilee, and walked the road to Jericho together. Their names served to remind them of their relationship to others. The ritual of naming is about building relationships with people.

A friend tells of his grandfather who was always talking about the Longs, who lived two doors away. The Longs had fourteen kids. Mrs. Long always looked tired. When she would come over to the grandfather's house, he would ask her: "How many children do you have?" Mrs. Long would name each of them and then give the total: fourteen. Although Mrs. Long gave him the number, she arrived at her response by remembering the faces and names of each.

This ritual of naming also permits people in a congregation to be caricatured, to be larger than life in the midst of the congregational family. The pastor may be named as well. Humor—being able to laugh at oneself—is necessary because often the name is derived from an embarrassing situation. One pastor told of her first tureen dinner in the new church. After dinner was over she went out to the kitchen to help the clean-up crew. When the work was completed she hopped up on the counter to sit and chat awhile. Her aim was a little off, though, and she landed on the remainder of Mrs. Schmidt's cake. Fortunately, her good humor prevailed and she laughed along with the kitchen crew. If the pastor can laugh and accept the name, the congregation and pastor live on and grow together.

Within the congregation are many persons who have been re-named by the community. Standing in an olive wood store in Bethlehem, a man pointed to an older woman across the room and said, "That's Angel. We call her that because she does more good in our church and community than anyone." These names are birthed out of community experiences. When the naming is announced, it is probably a part of the adoption process. Once you have your family name, you become a full member of the community.

7. Counting faces

"What is the size of your congregation?" I asked Joanne. "Well, now, let me count," she responded, and name by name Joanne called forth the faces. Small churches are about faces and names of persons who are considered part of the family. Some-times they are members, and sometimes they are not. Often people in the community consider Valley Chapel their church without ever formally joining.

In speaking of these rituals, clergy need to be aware of what is really happening during these times when rituals are being lived out. Paying attention to those persons who did not speak or at-tend is often as important as remembering those who did. Plac-ing a phone call to say, "Trudy, I missed you tonight at the meeting—I hope you are feeling all right," is often helpful in let-ting folks know they were missed.

8. Waiting and beginning

This ritual is about knowing when it is time to begin. One pas-tor explains: "We don't always start at eleven o'clock because we know that Dean will be bringing his mother in a wheelchair and Harold will be bringing his mother, who uses a walker. If they are not here, someone knows either why they aren't coming to church or that they are. If they are coming, we wait for them."

That congregation knows about the ritual of waiting and be-ginning: worship begins when the folks gather—whenever that time is. The small-church members are accountable to each other as family. This is why waiting is important. And waiting is im-portant to the pastor, because beginning at the wrong time can jeopardize the pastor's position and place her or him outside the family.

9. Blessing the space

I once worked with a small community of Roman Catholic religious leaders. At one of our weekend gatherings we stood together outside the conference room where we were to meet and asked God to bless the space we were about to enter. Only then did we enter the room, now a blessed space for us to gather for our meetings.

Rituals of blessing space keep us attentive to who we are and what we are about. In our homes we find a space for our favorite pictures, whether they fit or not. Until certain items are in place, the space is a house rather than a home. The pastor will be asked to bless a variety of significant spaces. The most obvious space is the church building, especially the sanctuary, but others include the parsonage or manse, members' homes, and certain key places in the community, such as the cemetery or the local park.

When a new pastor arrives in a community, moving into a residence is one ritual of blessing space. Certain rituals help a congregation to know that the pastor is "in and settled." When Evelyn moved into the parsonage, she mentioned that the church members transformed one of the bedrooms into a study for her by opening up an old closet and building shelves for her books. Her response was clearly enthusiastic: "I'm happy to be here, and the closet library is lovely!" Being able to find the positive elements in a new situation and work with them plays a major role in being adopted by the new community. How a pastor receives her or his living space is intricately tied to "blessing the space."

10. Place

The silent ritual of place is about territory and turf. Who goes into the kitchen and who does not, who sits in what pew and who does not—all have to do with the ritual of place. The matriarch or patriarch of the congregation usually sits somewhere in the middle of the sanctuary. One matriarch who moved from Pennsylvania to Illinois successfully managed her place in the congregation through the telephone and mail service. Although physically absent, she remained indisputably "in place" as the central decision-maker of the congregation.

"Pew guards" are self-appointed folks who cling to the aisle seats. New persons are often intimidated by these aisle-sitters as they try to crawl over them getting to the empty pew spaces. Pew guards do not move; they challenge folks to get over them as a silent ritual of place.

The place of the doorkeeper is by the door, watching for new people. Often the doorkeepers are central to the adoption process, as are the matriarch and patriarch. They are central because they have been around long enough to know the history. When the sermon begins, some doorkeepers step out into the fresh air and continue the watch for any newcomers.

Empty places in a church building are not really empty places. One Sunday a new visitor came to Harmony Church. He walked down the aisle, crawled over the pew guard, and slid into the place of Mrs. Harry Robinson. She died fifteen years ago, but the members all knew where she sat, and they leave the space empty for her. New folks can sit to either side of her place, but not on the saint. The communion of the saints is alive and well in the small church!

Implications for Ministry

Silent rituals remind us that all is not clearly spelled out in ministry. Folks have certain ways of doing things that are not written down but are continually emerging with time. Ministry is a dance in which we improvise and create out of what we know. No one person leads, although there is a lot of room for participation from the pastor. The pastor needs to be sensitive and alert to when it is time to listen and learn and when it is time to lead and speak.

"I went to the Bellflower congregation prepared for a ministry of program. That's what I knew. They don't want program. They want to gather together as the family of God on Sunday," says Pastor Evelyn. The expectation of many new pastors is that program is central to congregational life in the small church. It is not. Ritual is more central than program. If a pastor has no knowledge of the rituals that renew and energize a congregation, then there is little possibility that that congregation will be renewed or energized.

It is a challenge to identify the rituals that are valued by the congregation. "I always walk to the back of the church after the benediction. I stand there alone sometimes because they're all busy with each other," explains one pastor. Since standing and greeting is a part of everyone's role in the small church, this pastor's ritual, which used to work in another church, must be put aside and another ritual, joining in with the greetings of the congregation, taken on.

Another challenge to clergy is to observe newly emerging rituals and to participate in their creation. Author Barbara Walker suggests that "perhaps it is not merely fortuitous that the word *ritual* is contained in the word *spiritual*. Sense of the sacred is contained in the human spirit, and in human actions, and in human desires. If rituals make these matters clear, then one of their greatest goals has been achieved."[18]

Questions for Reflection and Conversation

1. What are the rituals that shape ministry in your congregation?

2. Who are the people who are telling you and others the stories of the history and tradition of your church? What role do they play in the congregation?

3. Identify those specific times when you were aware that members of the congregation were considering adopting you. Have you been adopted by the church?

4. How have you blessed space in the congregation, your home, the community?

5. Identify the ritual names in your church, and when and where you heard the names for the first time.

6. How do you participate in silent rituals? Identify who is present in the ritual and how you can participate.

Chapter 4

Parish
World-View

According to James F. Hopewell, author of *Congregation: Stories and Structures*, world-views reflect and give a focus to group experience, providing a map within which words and actions make sense.[1] Each congregation has a prevailing world-view, and this world-view affects the way the congregation sees itself and the world around it. Difficulties can develop when the pastor and the congregation hold different world-views, so it can be important to identify and understand what world-views are and their implications for ministry.

A parish's world-view is the predominant way a congregation sees, experiences, and responds to the world. In the activities and life of a congregation stories are told, traditions are honored, narrative is recounted, and persons begin to unfold their understanding of the world in which they live. They live in their world and live out of their view of the world. Each congregation tends to interpret the world in a particular way, to have one dominant world-view, but there are also people in the pews who tell their stories from other world-views.

World-view affects the way sermons are heard, stories are received, and the future of the church is discussed. World-view stories are told during times of acute crisis. Hopewell states:

> The setting of a congregation is the order by which its gossip, sermons, strategies, and fights—the household idiom—gain their reasonableness. . . . Tales in a local church tend to travel in packs: one good story evokes another, one member's account of an illness, for example, is usually reciprocated in kind. In comradeship and commiseration members top each

other's stories, building up the world setting that they together inhabit.[2]

Each congregation arranges its view of the world by the stories it tells. By listening to the stories, we are able to hear where a congregation positions itself in its view of the world.

Pastors come to a congregation with a way to view the world that has been molded by their own lives and by their congregations of origin. In paying attention to the parish's world-view, they can gain insights into conflicts and disruptions that are rooted in conflicting world-views. Pastors often take responsibility for conflicted situations that actually have nothing to do with the pastor but have a great deal to do with internal differences in the way the congregation and the pastor view the world.

One way to envision world-view is to "consider a church building made largely of windows that permit the building's occupants to look out four sides to a continuous horizon. Now picture that horizon to be a gigantic circle of Western literature."[3] If members were to enter this transparent building and position themselves at their window of choice, it is highly unlikely that they would be scattered all over the circle; rather, they would probably be grouped together.

In addition to those of James Hopewell, the works of Northrop Frye are also helpful in understanding parish world-view. Frye describes the great circle of Western literature as four points on the total horizon: east, south, west, and north. If the members of a congregation were to arrange themselves according to Frye's horizon, they would "arrange themselves to face a particular point on the circle."[4] Every person holds one of these four world-views as dominant, and each congregation positions itself as a whole through the stories it tells. Knowing where the congregation and leaders are may ease our journey of ministry.

Frye's great circle of Western literature suggests that we convey one of four primary images in our stories: comedy (east), romance (south), tragedy (west), and irony and satire (north). Hopewell's corresponding images are gnostic, charismatic, canonic, and empiric. Each of the four world-views is non-hierarchical. None is better than or more significant than another: each just has a distinct way of looking at the world.

The world-view chart shows a combination of Frye's and Hopewell's circle of four world-views. According to this chart, ironic and romantic are opposites, and tragic and comic are opposites. Hopewell observed that when people were told stories

Parish World-View Chart

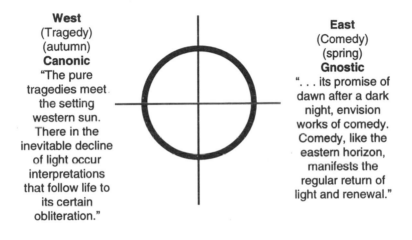

North
(Irony and Satire)
(winter)
Empiric
"Put the ironies in the northern night and cold. What
gives life in the ironic North is not cosmic certainty but
a sense of common unheroic humanity."

West
(Tragedy)
(autumn)
Canonic
"The pure
tragedies meet
the setting
western sun.
There in the
inevitable decline
of light occur
interpretations
that follow life to
its certain
obliteration."

East
(Comedy)
(spring)
Gnostic
". . . its promise of
dawn after a dark
night, envision
works of comedy.
Comedy, like the
eastern horizon,
manifests the
regular return of
light and renewal."

South
(Romance)
(summer)
Charismatic
". . . pure romantic interpretations. In the bright
sun and sharp shadows of a southern exposure,
romance pits innocent good against obvious evil
in high noon adventure."[5]

from a world-view that was opposite from their own personal
world-view, they were often not able to understand them, and
they had little patience with those who were telling these stories.

Learning from the Circle of World-Views

James Hopewell based much of his study of parish world-
views on his personal experience of visits to his hospital bedside
as he was battling cancer. Hopewell died in 1984, leaving a third
draft of his book, which Barbara G. Wheeler from Auburn Semi-

nary completed. The basic core of his theory of congregations is that "congregational culture is not an accidental accumulation of symbolic elements but a coherent system whose structural logic is *narrative.*"[6] The stories of a congregation carry clues concerning its parish world-view. By listening, remembering, and asking questions, the parish world-view unfolds.

Hopewell suggests specific places where the prevailing world-view of the congregation is usually able to be perceived. They include jokes, stories, lore, the written material of the parish, conversations that follow administrative meetings, sermons, classroom presentations, use of space, organizations, social groupings, processes of membership, lines of authority and influence, use of time, ritual, social class, demographic features, history, conscious and unconscious symbols, and conflict.[7] Hearing world-view is a careful task of listening and observing the congregation's and the pastor's language.

Discerning a person's or congregation's world-view can be confusing, so Hopewell developed a world-view test instrument to determine the world-view held by church members. Respondents were to complete the statement, selecting the statement that best reflected their view. When Hopewell asked several questions to different congregations, he found some typical responses. From these responses he was able to discern the person's predominant world-view.

Each of the four positions on the world-view circle speaks of the world and how to live in the world through the telling of stories. There is a seasonal cycle of spring, summer, autumn, and winter in the great circle of stories. World-view is not always pure and clear, however. At times it appears that the storyteller is standing between two world-views.

Comic/Gnostic

The comic/gnostic world-view is not humorous, but it does include the basic elements of comedy. The elements of comedy as described by Frye include a movement from one kind of society to another and a hero who overcomes obstacles to complete the cycle with a comic resolution. Parties or festive rituals accompany the new society. Often the festivity is in the form of a wedding. There is no question that life in this story is basically good. It may not be full of humorous incidents, but it has a happy ending.[8]

When Hopewell discusses the comic/gnostic world-view, he talks about stories that begin with a problem and move to a solution. These stories begin with a state of crisis created by "some illusion," which then move to a "harmonious recovery brought about by discovering the true nature of the circumstances." These stories end in "unions—pacts, embraces, marriages—that symbolize the ultimately trustworthy working of the world."[9] Each story has a meaning that is hidden but eventually unfolds before us.

When hospital chaplains and interns with this world-view came to Hopewell's hospital bedside, their words of encouragement were to "get with your cancer." Their intent was for Hopewell to learn how "lifesaving self-awareness techniques" can be used to understand the connection between mental stress and growing cancer.[10] Their words were meant to offer a way of recovery, for knowing more about the illness and the way possible cures occur would increase the potential of the patient recovering from the disease.

The language accompanying the comic/gnostic world-view includes phrases such as "it all adds up," "it will all work out," "let go and let God," "possibility thinking," "go with the flow," "holistic healing practices," and so on.[11] The sick will be told, "Get with your illness and understand you can help yourself," or "Realize the divine potential within and you can turn this illness around."

The endings of comic/gnostic stories are upbeat. Some of the responses to Hopewell's world-view test for this particular world-view included, "I see my religion as insight into my own spark of divinity" and "When I die I may later be reincarnated."[12] Stories from a comic/gnostic world-view are about how the parish survived some terrible circumstance—the flood of 1982, the unemployment at the plant, the economic crisis in our community. The studies usually end with comments such as, "In fact, the church actually is better off because we leaned on each other in this town." The true meaning is always just beneath the surface of these stories, and in God's time we come to understand exactly what that true meaning is. Comic/gnostic conversations include encouraging folks to wait and not to jump to premature conclusions.

The biblical story of Joseph being sold into slavery in Egypt illustrates the comic/gnostic world-view. The story begins with a problem: Joseph was one of seven brothers. His father favored Joseph and had a coat of many colors made for him. His brothers were so jealous that they conspired to sell him and tell their father that Joseph was dead. Many years later the brothers were sent to Egypt to buy corn because there was a famine in the land. However, when Joseph's brothers came to Egypt to buy corn, Joseph recognized them but kept his identity from being revealed. The brothers were imprisoned as spies and requested to bring forth their younger brother. Over time Joseph made his true identity known to his brothers. The hidden meaning was revealed, and the story had a happy ending.

Comic/gnostic world-view stories begin with a problem and end with a solution. The hero works through the obstacles created in the story. Hidden meaning is revealed, and the resolution is a happy one.

Romantic/Charismatic

If we move to the "sunny south," to the romantic/charismatic world-view, we encounter, according to Frye, a wish-fulfillment dream,[13] an extraordinarily persistent nostalgia searching for "some golden age in time or space." There is romance in adventure in this search for the perfect age, a quest that involves three stages. The first stage is a conflict that includes a perilous journey with minor adventures. There is a struggle with death in the second stage. The final stage is the discovery, which includes the exaltation of the hero.

For Hopewell, romantic/charismatic world-view stories emphasize recovery through a spiritual adventure. There are experiences of good and evil, and the protagonists and antagonists are clearly differentiated. The hero is on a perilous journey and in that journey the self moves to the supernatural. The ordinary laws of nature are suspended and special courage and incredible endurance become natural. The expectation is for a direct experience of God's power. The constancy of God is claimed.[14]

Language such as "Miracles happen, and we in the church are praying that God will work a miracle in you" and "Through this experience you will grow in Christ, and you'll be a better Christian because of it" are natural for this world-view. Folks who told the romantic/charismatic hospital bedside stories to Hopewell during his illness were seminary students and some members of his parish. Their stories suggested, "God has something special in mind for you. If you continue to believe in the Bible and God's power and love, God will perform a miracle in your life." There is always an opportunity in the illness for God to love in a surprising way.

When Hopewell questioned respondents from the romantic/ charismatic world-view, he heard these replies: "I see my religion as filled with the Holy Spirit" and "When I die I keep the blessings God has already begun to give me."[15] In this world-view, special courage is needed to endure the journey, but at the end of the perilous journey God's blessing will be received. Biblical miracle stories, such as the restoration of sight to Bartimaeus, suggest a world-view that surely Jesus will come and heal. Even in the crowd, somehow, some way, Jesus will be able to see the sick and heal them.

Tom, a pastor, was diagnosed with cancer. We all prayed for him. Our prayers were for healing of this disease. At one point in his radiation treatments, it was questionable whether or not Tom would live. His loss of hair and weight were so drastic that his entire appearance had changed. Once he came to a staff meeting and some of us did not know who he was. The drastic physical appearance did not discourage the romantic/charismatic world-view holders, though. They continued to believe that God would intervene. After two years of fighting the cancer, Tom resumed his ministry. Each time we meet, there is an acknowledgment of the miracle God performed in his life.

The romantic/charismatic world-view storyteller believes that somewhere in the hero's journey something will turn the story from despair to wholeness. Some supernatural intervention and spiritual adventure will bring about recovery.

Tragic/Canonic

The harsh world brings death, but it also brings the promise of salvation through death. In the tragic/canonic world-view, the "tragic hero is not cured but saved, by an identification with the transcendent pattern of tragic life."[16] Ultimate happiness is not for this life but will be on the other side of this life. Since tragedy exists and life decays, it is necessary to sacrifice the self before resolution can occur. "You must follow God's plan for you," "Remember that you will be with Christ," and "If everybody did God's will this would not happen" are common expressions of this world-view.

The tragic/canonic world-view moves from solution to problem, which is the opposite of the comic world-view. When a congregation speaks from the tragic/canonic world-view, it portrays Christ as a tragic hero who accepts the cross without an intervention. Obedience is essential to the tragic/canonic world-view. The adventure stories told by the romantic are left behind, as this world-view is fated for catastrophe, "fulfilling the pattern laid down in Holy Scriptures and ancient teachings."

Frye speaks of tragic heroes as "wrapped in the mystery of their communion with that something beyond which we can only see through them, and which is the source of their strengths and their fate alike. . . . The tragic hero leaves his servants to do his 'living' for him, and the center of tragedy is in the hero's isolation. . . . The tragic hero is our mediator with God."[17]

The tragic/canonic world-view storyteller sees the world pattern through an "authoritative interpretation . . . often considered God's revealed word."[18] Hopewell found that this hospital bedside world-view conversation was offered by family members and fellow ministers: "My tragic friends and I would honestly mark changes in my life and track its heroic descent into darkness. . . . What my family and clergy friends emphasized in their stories was not the sweet fulfillment of our own desires but our recognition of God's laws governing our own short lives."[19]

When persons holding this world-view responded to Hopewell's questions, they stated, "I see my religion as born again in Christ," and "When I die, I shall then be with Christ."[20] "Bible-centered, Bible-believing churches," "get right with God," references to "moral decay and damnation" are all part of the language spoken when the tragic/canonic world-view is embraced. The romantic hero meets God through personal encounter. The tragic hero meets God through God's Word and will.[21]

Ironic/Empiric

The ironic/empiric world-view relies on objective, verifiable data obtained through one's own five senses. This world-view rejects the intervention of the supernatural. The Holy Scripture is analyzed as historical data rather than accepted as revealed truth. For those holding the ironic world-view, life is unjust, and miracles do not happen. Bad things *do* happen to good people. They trust only in realism. The reality of life is that all of humanity is in the same plight.[22]

Wade Clark Roof, professor of sociology at the University of Massachusetts, Amherst, uses the term "cosmopolitan religion," to describe this group's values. As Roof points out, the ironic/empiric parishioners are those faithful church members whose "religion affirms (a) the centrality of ethical principles in their meaning systems; (b) a parsimony of beliefs, few attributes of numinosity; (c) breadth of perspective; (d) piety defined as a personal search for meaning; and (e) license to doubt."[23]

Ironic/empiric world-view stories were told at Hopewell's bedside primarily by fellow faculty members. These visitors avoided the sadness of the tragedy, looked realistically at the "scientific therapies that might stave off death," and focused upon the medical prognosis. "In our fellowship many touched me and some prayed. Their prayers were narratives that anticipated the skill of the medical staff and our emotional well-being. As a brother caught in an incongruous world, I was, by their efforts, loved but not led to healing."[24] "This illness may take your life," "the breakthroughs in research are just not able to cure this disease," and "I don't know why God permits such terrible things to happen" is the language of the ironic/empiric storyteller.

Holders of this world-view completed Hopewell's world-view test questions by stating, "I see my religion as 'not holier than thou,'" and "When I die, I may or may not live afterward."[25] Being honest and realistic, acceptance of illness or catastrophe as a fact of life, and giving attention to issues of justice are the phrases that convey an ironic sense of the world.[26] Those holding this world-view are apt to say, "That's just the way it is. . . ."

Implications for Ministry

In ministering in the small church, pastors are challenged to listen for their parish's world-view. Each story and storyteller will offer clues to understanding ministry. Being called by God, responding to God's call, and being privileged to live with folks in a faith community requires careful listening. Ministry in the small church is complicated, layered, and historically rooted in traditions and rituals that are oral rather than written, more learned in community than transmitted by seminary lectures. Identifying a congregation's dominant world-view requires an attentiveness to the way folks see themselves in their world and the way they participate in that world. Most of all, ministry and world-view are united in story. When we hear, translate, and act on world-view, we do so through the hearing of story.

Hopewell's intense study of congregational life uncovered the truth that we gather with folks who make us feel comfortable. There is a congregational culture that is created around narrative. One scenario for clergy and congregation is that they might speak the same language of world-view. The reality is that in congregations there is more than one view held, articulated and lived. The challenge of ministry is fourfold: to develop the ability to hear our world-view and the world-view of the congregation; to distinguish a common ground to hear and to be heard by others; to be aware that our world-view preference may shade the way we welcome newcomers, create ministry, bring in and exclude others from community; and to stretch our hearing and our speaking when opposite world-views are present.

If the clergy and congregation hold opposite world-views, what then? As in any situation of opposites, there are several steps that can be taken. Begin with what you have in common and hold important in your life and work together. Then find the common space that you share as essential. Third, determine what parts of your work are most bothersome. Fourth, agree to disagree on some items. Fifth, recognize and articulate together the different ways of seeing the same issue. Finally, find ways to work on the critical issues while respecting your differing opinions.

There are no magic wands to wave over dissension and disagreement. The worst-case scenario is that in such situations we forget to examine the cycles we are entangled in and consequently we never break the cycle. But by paying careful attention to the way the world-views of the pastor and the congregation influence and affect the decisions, activities, and expectations of the parish, we can gain insight into solutions and resolutions for conflicts.

The ministry quilt is padded with layers of batting that are not just thin layers of the quilt—they are "the stuff" that makes a quilt a quilt. Examining the world-view of pastor and parishioner means opening the layers of the quilt for a history lesson on how we came to use this particular fabric for our particular quilt.

Questions for Reflection and Conversation

1. What prevailing world-view do you hear present in your congregation when parishioners tell their stories? If this notion is new to you, begin to listen to the stories and identify what you hear.

2. What parish world-view do you favor?

3. What prevailing parish world-view is spoken by the lay leaders?

4. Look at the three world-views you have identified in questions 1, 2, and 3. Are these world-views the same, opposites, or

a combination? What insights do you have on the communication patterns and potential conflicts among these three groupings?

5. What are some of the ways you can begin to address the diversity you experience and observe in your congregation, based on your understanding of world-views that differ?

Epilogue

"I don't stitch anymore. When I was a volunteer, I stitched, but I was aware of how uncomfortable it was for some more traditional leaders."

This pastor was aware that her leadership style was being shaped by an expectation that was not necessarily compatible with her natural leadership style. She adjusted to the norm but was delighted when she heard the female traits in leadership that are not the traditional way of leading being discussed.

This book is intended to assist clergy and church leaders in identifying how through careful attention to qualities of leadership, the spiritual life, rituals, and world view we can see and hear the conversations present in our parishes. By placing these four transparent overlays on our own experience, we can gain insight into ways we in our ministries can be more effective.

The future of clergy in the small church may prove to be very encouraging. The future of every church is rooted in its particular history, a history in which it can find strength and uniqueness and the capacity to change. Leaders must see beyond what we have always done and been to consider how we can respond to God's call for us in the future.

Moving into the future with congregations that are historically tied to tradition and "the way we have always been" is quite a challenge. Given the flexibility needed for leadership in the years ahead, and given the discontinuity surrounding us, it is imperative that clergy cultivate the capacity for juggling multiple roles.

My hope is that this book has opened to you some of the world views and rituals that are often present in the small church. One pastor who came to my clergywomen leadership seminar took me aside and said, "As a male, I have resisted some of the qualities you described. I know I have. They seemed counter to what I had been taught. I now see the advantage and hope I can be free to use them."

Pastors have different styles of leadership, all of which can be effective in ministry. There is not one right way to lead. God calls, and our response is to be who God has called us to be. We must bring our gifts to the table and know that we have some, but not all, of the gifts.

The words below came from a pastor as she reflected on her ministry in the small church:

> I've preached on what others may have been afraid to tell
>   . . . in telling the truth
>   . . . I had to be careful to tell *my* truth.
>   . . . ministry produces a kind of humility
>   . . . I know that I am dispensable.
>
> Pastors are a means to an end
>   . . . you being here in this space for ministry
>   . . . you can watch ministry flow through people
>
> It clarifies why I am there.
> I am the minister of Word and sacrament
>
> Ministry is a divesting of yourself
>   . . . all the time.
>
> It's very freeing
>   . . . it gives me the chance to do what I think ministry is
>   all about
>   . . . making very concrete the love of God in their lives
>   . . . so they can take charge of their lives.
>
> It's a lot like raising children
>   . . . if they don't want me to tie their shoes
>   . . . I don't.
>
> It's scary as hell.[1]

Endnotes

Chapter 1

1. John Naisbitt and Patricia Aburdene, *Reinventing the Corporation* (New York: Warner Books, 1985), 242. Also quoted in Helgesen, 40.

2. Ibid., 241.

3. Patricia Aburdene and John Naisbitt, *Megatrends for Women: Women Are Changing the World* (London: Century Random House), 1993.

4. Sally Helgesen, *The Female Advantage: Women's Ways of Leading* (New York: Doubleday/Currency, 1990), 28.

5. Ibid., 18.

6. Ibid., 19–28.

7. Ibid., 27.

8. For reading on the small church as a single-cell, primary group see Carl S. Dudley, *Making the Small Church Effective* (Nashville: Abingdon Press, 1978), chp. 2.

9. Nancy T. Foltz, ed., *Religious Education in the Small Membership Church* (Birmingham, Ala.: Religious Education Press, 1990). The wall chart is included in the back of the book, and the six sizes of churches are discussed in chapter 1.

10. Wendy Whiteside and Linda Reed Brown, "Festival of Sharing: A Great Way for Small Churches to Cooperate," *The Small Church Newsletter of the Missouri School of Religion,* Vol. 2, No. 3 (September 1991), 6.

11. "An Ecumenical Parish Success Story," *The Small Church Newsletter of the Missouri School of Religion,* Vol. 2, No. 1 (March 1991), 3, 7.

12. Helgesen, 25.

13. Sister Sheila Carney addressed the Sisters of Mercy at Carlow College, Pittsburgh, Pennsylvania, in October 1990.

14. Tex Sample, *U. S. Lifestyles and Mainline Churches: A Key to Reaching People in the Nineties* (Louisville, Ky.: Westminster/John Knox Press, 1990).

15. Sample, 93.

16. Helgesen, xx–xxi.

17. See wall chart in Foltz, *Religious Education in the Small Membership Church*.

18. Telephone conversation with Douglas A. Walrath, April 23, 1992.

Chapter 2

1. Martha A. Robbins, *Midlife Women and Death of Mother* (New York: Peter Lang, 1990), 77.

2. Mary Catherine Bateson, *Composing a Life* (New York: Penguin, 1990), 34.

3. Charles Handy, *The Age of Unreason* (Boston: Harvard Business School Press, 1990), 46.

4. Ibid., 178.

5. Sharon Parks, *The Critical Years* (San Francisco: Harper and Row, 1986), 24.

6. Gerhard Wehr, *Jung: A Biography* (Boston: Shambhala, 1988), 165–166.

7. Wehr, 172–173.

8. Robert Bly, *Iron John: A Book About Men* (Reading, Mass.: Addison-Wesley, 1990), 209–210.

9. From a conversation with Rick Wellock, a planner and educator with The McNellis Company, October 2, 1991.

10. Bateson, 54.

11. Address to the congregation at the Chapter of Elections as the Mother Superior by Sister Sheila Carney, Pittsburgh, Pennsylvania, January 18, 1991.

12. Quoted in Bateson, 178.

Chapter 3

1. Barbara G. Walker, *Women's Rituals* (New York: Harper San Francisco, 1990), vii–viii.

2. William Willimon and Robert L. Wilson, *Preaching and Worship in the Small Church* (Nashville, Abingdon, 1980), 79–91.

3. Questions 1–3 are adapted from W. S. F. Pickering, *Durkheim's Sociology of Religion Themes and Theories* (London: Routledge and Kegan Paul, 1984), 325.

4. Hans J. Mol, *Identity and the Sacred* (New York: The Free Press, 1976), 233.

5. Pickering, 330–334.

6. Ibid., 331.

7. Ibid., 335–339.

8. Ibid., 354.

9. Ibid., 336.

10. Barbara Hargrove, *The Sociology of Religion: Classical and Contemporary Approaches*, second edition (Arlington Heights, Ill.: Harland Davidson, Inc., 1989), 50.

11. Mol, 236–237.

12. Leonel L. Mitchell, *The Meaning of Ritual* (New York: Paulist Press, 1977), 136–137.

13. Pickering, 34.
14. Mol, 13.
15. Pickering, 324.
16. Ibid., 424.
17. Mircea Eliade, *Birth and Rebirth: The Religious Meanings of Initiation in Human Culture* (New York: Harper and Brother, 1958), as quoted in S. P. Nagendra, *The Concept of Ritual in Modern Sociological Theory* (Nagendra, India: The Academic Journals of India, 1971), 29.
18. Walker, 9.

Chapter 4

1. James F. Hopewell, *Congregation: Stories and Structures* (Philadelphia: Fortress Press, 1989), 85.
2. Ibid.
3. Jackson W. Carroll, Carl S. Dudley, William McKinney, eds., *Handbook for Congregational Studies* (Nashville: Abingdon Press, 1992), 32–33. For further study in the area of congregational images on world view, see Carl S. Dudley and Sally A. Johnson, *Energizing the Congregation: Images that Shape Your Congregation's Ministry* (Louisville: Westminster, 1993).
4. Hopewell, 58.
5. Ibid., 67.
6. Ibid., xii.
7. Ibid., 89.
8. Northrop Frye, *Anatomy of Criticism: Four Essays* (Princeton: Princeton University Press, 1957), 163–167.
9. Hopewell, 58.
10. Hopewell, 59.
11. Carroll, 33.
12. Hopewell, 94.
13. Frye, 186–197
14. Hopewell, 80.
15. Ibid., 94.
16. Ibid., 61.
17. Frye, 207–208.
18. Hopewell, 69.
19. Ibid., 60.
20. Ibid., 94.
21. Carroll, 33.
22. Hopewell, 61.
23. Ibid., 82.
24. Ibid., 61.
25. Ibid., 94.
26. Carroll, 34.

Epilogue

1. This material came from a conversation with Rev. Beverly James, Pittsburgh Theological Seminary, September 23, 1990.